What others are saying about Change Your Mind, Change Your Life: **Work on Your Own Terms**, In Midlife & Beyond.

Jan is conscientious, passionate, enlightened, knowledgeable and, as a "blooming boomer," is living her message. Facing those fears that hold most of us back, she is following her passion—to help others find fulfillment in a new life-work direction—maximizing potential in midlife and beyond. Inspirational, practical, directional, thought-provoking and encouraging. This book has been written just in time for me (and for you)!

Liz McKnight, Art Therapist, MEd, DVATI, BCATR
www.lizmcknight.com

Brimming with inspirational quotes and personal insights from the author's twenty years as a career counsellor, Work On Your Own Terms *is an enjoyable and motivational tool for people of any age contemplating a career move.*

Darlene Mace, Real Estate Agent, Coast Realty Group
www.GabriolaLiving.com

A plastic brain, quantum physics, and unlimited opportunity—oh my! I never thought my future would look so bright. Jan Moore dares us to explore our fears of breaking out of the status quo and gives us a practical guide to living a meaningful life filled with passion. Her book is quirky, punchy, out of the box, and thoroughly enjoyable. I only wish I had read this in my twenties!

Janet McDonald, Life Coach, Career Counsellor (CCDP), Artist
www.empowerlifedreams.com
http://janetmcdonald.artistwebsites.com

At least 10 percent of all profit from this book will be shared with two organizations, one international, and one local.

KIVA
Kiva is a non-profit microfinance organization. For as little as $25, you can help alleviate poverty for borrowers from around the world. Your donation can help women to start their own businesses, improve their lives, and achieve their dreams.

If you look at Kiva, people with a very modest amount of money can make a huge positive impact all around the world.

Bill Clinton, former US president

Loans that change lives.   www.KIVA.com

The Gabriola Commons
The Commons is a community-owned common area in the heart of Gabriola Island. It has a covenant, the first in Canada, that guarantees its long-term protection. It is focused on agriculture and meeting the social needs of our community.

Through time, and in all places, the commons has been, and remains, that which we share collectively. It's the gifts we've inherited—from nature, from human knowledge and from cultures that came before us. And it is our gift to future generations.

Shelagh Huston, community activist

The Gabriola Commons . . . a place for everyone.
www.GabriolaCommons.ca

Change Your Mind, Change Your Life:
Work On Your Own Terms
In Midlife & Beyond

by Janine L. Moore

Change Your Mind, Change Your Life: **Work On Your Own Terms,** *In Midlife & Beyond*

Library and Archives Canada Cataloguing in Publication

Moore, Janine L., 1953-, author
      Work on your own terms : in midlife & beyond / by Janine L. Moore.

At head of title: Change your mind, change your life.
Includes bibliographical references.
Issued in print and electronic formats.
ISBN 978-0-9917985-0-6 (pbk.).--ISBN 978-0-9917985-1-3 (pdf)

      1. Quality of work life. 2. Fear. 3. Career changes. I. Title.

HD6955.M66 2013   650.1   C2013-906611-X
                                                C2013-906612-8

This book is dedicated to you, Dear Reader.

It is designed to move you to take action,
so you really can live and work on your own terms.

I don't just want you to read it.
I want you to live it!

Acknowledgements

This book is a synthesis of the thoughts and ideas of many people. It was, in many ways, written by everyone whose writing I have read or whose voice I have heard. It has been influenced by the work of writers, career counsellors, career changers, entrepreneurs, artists, friends, and family.

I give special credit to two female mentors, Barbara J. Winter and Barbara Sher. Both these women have inspired me to reach for my dreams. I will be forever grateful to them.

Special thanks also go to Liz, Doug, Dar, and Keltie who read my early drafts and gave valuable feedback and suggestions. Thanks to my husband, Tony Bridge, the photographer who provided the cover photos and supported my decision to devote so much time to writing—and to my little dog, Newman, who was at my side most of the time reminding me to take fresh air breaks by taking him for a walk. Thanks also go to Janet and Kirsten who were with me when the seed for this book was first planted and then grew into my "Plan B."

Huge gratitude goes out to the entire Team at Aurora Publishing who helped me every step along the way: Kathleen, inspiration extraordinaire; wonderful designers, Nik and Tara; and my thankfully detail-oriented and patient editor, Jens.

The bibliography credits the authors I came across while doing my research—but there are many others who, over the years, have also influenced me. This list is naturally, but regrettably, incomplete. I give thanks to them as well.

Table of Contents

Table of Contents

And the day came when the risk to remain tight in a bud was more painful than the risk it took to blossom.

Anais Nin

Chapter 1:
Overview - What's It All About?

We cannot live the afternoon of life according to the program of life's morning, for what was great in the morning will be little at evening, and what in the morning was true will at evening have become a lie.

Carl G. Jung

Want to know how to undo the shackles and get yourself out of "job jail"? This book will take you from where you are now to where you want to be.

There are many midlife career changers who have already joined the huge wave of positive change. Come aboard. The water is warm and inviting, and the sun has never shone brighter. You'll enjoy the ride.

In his often-quoted book, *Think and Grow Rich*, Napoleon Hill first identified the six primary fears that tend to hold people back. They are the same fears clients have expressed to me during career counselling sessions: fear of

- poverty
- criticism
- poor health
- loss of love
- old age
- death

In this book, we'll address these fears head-on and see if we can change our perception of them. If we succeed in transforming negative feelings about these fears into positive ones, we will be able to change our lives and design the life we want to live. See if by the end of this book you agree with Joseph Campbell, who said, "The cave you fear to enter holds the treasure you seek."

Let's kick those fears to the curb, have a little fun while doing it, and replace them with a new perspective:

- having enough money to maintain your comfort level
- having little concern for the opinions of others
- recognizing the importance of work/life balance
- embracing the love of your life
- welcoming the wisdom of age
- focusing on the legacy you will leave behind

Baby, we've come a long way
In the 1960s, you thought about changing the world. Now that you've reached midlife, you really can—simply by changing your mindset.

Remember those "Question Authority!" buttons that were popular in the 1970s? A lot of Baby Boomers have rediscovered that button, especially when it comes to how they plan to continue working.

There are seven guidelines that form the undercurrent of *Work on Your Own Terms.*

Keep these in mind while reading this book:

1. Be willing to face your fears. Use obstacles as a challenge to generate creative solutions.

2. Take yourself out of your comfort zone. Don't be afraid of failure. That is how we learn what doesn't work for us.

3. Be persistent. Most people who are viewed as "overnight successes" spent years perfecting their craft. In today's quick-fix world, persistence may be the most difficult trait to master.

4. Get clear about why you want to work on your own terms. Focus on a compelling vision. In considering saving funds for your future, which would motivate you more?—Saving a large sum of money to pay for your care in a senior citizen home, or saving for an RV so you can travel across country while working on the road?

5. Create a picture of what you want. A Vision Board can be a useful tool for this. Some might prefer to create one on their computer using Pinterest. Remember to view your vision often.

6. Recognize that you have the power to make your own choices. Choosing to create your own future is empowering.

7. Commit to reaching your goals. Take a step today. Life is too short not to live your dreams. By midlife, it feels even shorter.

Do it now!

Keep this acronym in mind when you plan your future:

D = Desire—be clear about what you want.
R = Reduce your expenses in the short-term.
E = Engage your intuition, creativity and intention.
A = Awareness of your core values is essential.
M = Meaningful work is your focus.

How this book came to be

This book evolved from the conclusions I drew from conducting extensive interviews with twenty-one people for my Master's thesis, called *The Future of Work*. They were mostly Baby Boomers who had transitioned from employee to self-employment. More than half had voluntarily chosen self-employment instead of working as an employee. One person felt forced into it. Eight people felt it was partially a voluntary choice and partially involuntary, as they were unable to find suitable employment in their field.

I wanted to learn which form of employment was their preference. I expected the results to be fifty-fifty—with half of them preferring self-employment and the other half wanting to return to the security of a job with an employer. I couldn't have been more wrong! I was dumbfounded when not one of them wanted to return to work as an employee. This was in spite of the fact that many had taken a dramatic drop in income.

Fortified by their advice and experience, I too headed off in the direction of self-employment. It turned out to be harder for me to shake my "employee mentality" than I had anticipated. Since completing my Master's thesis in 1999, I have hopped back and forth between the two worlds of work—without fully committing to either of them.

The good news is that my familiarity with both worlds has informed the way I have encouraged career counselling clients to explore all of the many work options available. I know that how people choose to work is a very personal decision and involves a lot of competing factors, including having responsibilities that involve partners and children.

Findings from my research
The overriding theme throughout the interviews was that the participants stated repeatedly that they had made conscious choices throughout their transition from employee to self-employment, based on their values about both their lives and their work. All spoke of their decision to choose the "road less travelled" when deciding whether to continue working as an employee or to seek alternate types of work.

Here are a few sample quotes. To protect the privacy of the respondents, I have used only their initials.

K. C. said, "I am the master of my own destiny. Security is an inner state of mind. There are all kinds of opportunities out there—you just need to let go of finding a job with a resumé. Adaptability and flexibility are really important. It's a question of being adaptable and flexible enough to fill a need. It's not that work is disappearing—it's just that people are realizing that they don't need a "job" as much as they used to. I quit my last job and decided that never again would I work in a job that was not in alignment with my values."

B. P. said, "I think most people won't trust themselves to move forward with their ideas—because those ideas might be unconventional—and yet I think that what our society is crying out for is the unconventional. It's the opportunity to be more fully realized and to do work that is of greater good in the world."

T. S. said, "My work and life values are the same. Authenticity is very important to me. If it was just a job, I wouldn't be able to do it for long. I have to feel like there's some part of me connected to it."

What's happened since 1999?
What my interview subjects said in 1999 has proven prophetic.

Boomers are flocking to alternate types of employment, and the growth in self-employment has increased steadily. Many want to work more flexible hours. The most likely generation to be exploring self-employment is the Baby Boomers. This holds true in both Canada and the United States. The media is full of such reports.

A 2008–2009 Statistics Canada report shows the increase in self-employment was mainly due to people aged fifty-five plus, with 58 percent of the overall increase attributed to women. The American Bureau of Labor shows similar findings. In 2012, they reported a much higher rate of self-employment among older workers (Cahill et al., 2012; see also LaRochelle-Cote, 2010; Rix, 2012).

What's your perception got to do with it?
In her ground-breaking book, *My Stroke of Insight*, brain scientist Jill Bolte Taylor documents her road back to recovery after a massive stroke. Her remarkable discovery is that how we perceive the world is based on the way our brain has been wired from birth, and that we are capable of rewiring it. A major insight was her realization that the life she had been leading had really been "a figment of her own imagination."

Could this also be true for the rest of us? How can you use this knowledge to help yourself? This book will open a window to the workings of your mind and encourage you to allow some fresh ideas in.

We live in a world of illusions. Just as Toto revealed the Wizard of Oz behind the curtain, we can uncover the illusions we live with. This knowledge allows us to create our own reality.

Stroke victims are being encouraged to work with their damaged hand behind a mirror that reflects their working hand so as to trick their brain into thinking their damaged limb is whole again. This process helps rewire connections in the brain to gradually repair the damaged limb.

We can also rewire our brains to overcome limiting beliefs. If we think we can, we can. If we think we can't, we can't. You can make a successful career transition in midlife by believing you can. Perhaps the New Age notion, "Our thoughts create our reality," is not as crazy as we once believed. Could this be the key to unlocking the barriers that prevent people from fulfilling their potential and living the lives they are capable of living?

The current state of the world economy is shaking people's old beliefs. It is important to remember that a belief is only a thought you continue to think. We are only victims of circumstance if we believe we are.

Taylor stresses that because our brains are not hard-wired, as previously believed, we are not forced to keep repeating behaviours that do not serve us. We have the option to choose a different way of being simply by changing the way we perceive the world around us. Who we were in the past does not have to be who are in the present or will be in the future.

Our thoughts are powerful! One of the most celebrated minds is Albert Einstein, who said the most important decision you will ever make is whether you believe you live in a friendly universe or a hostile universe. That decision will colour your experience of life. Are you afraid of what the future will bring or are you excited about creating it? Creating your ideal future is the fun part!

Midlife changes us
After reaching midlife, our attention shifts toward our unexplored potential. We feel an inner drive to discover our true path. We just need to know how. If we have spent much of our life with other people directing our career path, we become disoriented about directing it ourselves.

Does it really matter what the unemployment rate is? You won't want most of the jobs available anyway. Boomers have grown tired of all the scare-mongering and headlines blasting us about our not having saved enough money for retirement. We're not retiring. We just want to work in a more fulfilling way that will feed both our body and soul.

It's no longer just about the money
It is *why* we work that is most important. It forms the heart of our passion and comes to the forefront in midlife. It is also our *why* that motivates us to save for the future. Our *why* is our purpose.

Work/Life balance has become a huge issue for Boomers. So many are juggling time spent at work, or *looking for work*, with caring for elderly parents or grandchildren, and have little time for personal interests. The stress can be enormous. Many clients arrived in my office at their breaking point, uncertain how to cope. Others wondered if they would ever have time to work at something they were truly passionate about. My workplace did not encourage clients to tap into their feelings and emotions, but I believe that is how we find the essence of who we are and why we are here. It is the road less travelled that needs to be explored to ensure an authentic life with a spiritual purpose.

Typical employment counselling spends most of the time looking at how to look for work rather than why we want to work. What larger purpose do we want to serve? Once we know that, it is easier to find out where the jobs are and how to get one. Increasingly though, Boomers have decided to create their own work.

The current trend shows self-employment as an attractive option for many of those aged fifty-five plus, especially for those with money in the bank. It's the most popular choice, but not the only one. This book reveals how to make your dreams come true even with fewer savings. You don't need to wait for better economic times. The price you pay to thwart your dreams can be much higher than the cost to implement them.

How this book is organized
Each chapter is broken down into bite-sized pieces so you have time to chew on and ponder its message. The focus is on how to

confront and work around the six main fears that hold people back.

The purpose of this book is to help you move forward with your dreams. While you are reading different perspectives on how others have chosen to live, you can select any elements that might work for you.

Each chapter ends with some action steps
Think of them as the puzzle pieces you are putting together to create your future. Do them even before you think you are ready. It will create the momentum needed to move you forward and connect you with those on a similar path.

You might want to devote a special journal to record your insights. Our beliefs are not static. They evolve over time. It is helpful to re-examine them whenever you become aware of a new perspective.

Do you enjoy your work?
When you enjoy your work, it contributes both emotional and physical well-being. It provides an opportunity to mix work with leisure, learning, and relaxation. If you don't plan on retiring, it makes sense to plan your future career now.

View this next stage of your life as a big adventure. It is a time to be who you were meant to be. It is also a time to give back to the world and to leave the legacy you want to leave.

Many of my midlife clients left jobs they didn't like and were struggling to locate another position they disliked less. Clients would get hired and then months or years later, they'd be back in my office wondering why the job had not been a good fit. If you find that something has been missing in your work life, read on. Midlife planning is about uncovering your identity, core values, and priorities. The government-funded employment services mandate allows little time to help clients with the self-reflection process.

When you are in job-search mode, you often experience one of two scenarios:

Scenario 1

You try to figure out how you can mold yourself to squeeze into someone else's job description. You search endlessly for jobs available on government job boards, in classified ads and on numerous websites. You network with everyone you meet. After six months, you may land a job using some of your skills. You might enjoy it, but the hours are inflexible and your employer decides when you will work, what you'll do, and how long you'll remain on the payroll.

Scenario 2

You decide to look at the barriers preventing you from living the life of your dreams. You assess the skills you truly enjoy using and identify what you are passionate about (work you would happily do for free if you didn't need the money). You then think about where you'd like to work, when and how— and offer those skills on a freelance basis. You may not earn a lot initially, but you are truly happy working at what you love. You are able to create your own hours and schedule vacation time around your workload. This is the option Boomers are leaning toward.

Which scenario will you choose? Will it be a little of each?

It is unhealthy to find a job and lose yourself in the process. There is a better way. Just as I would not encourage anyone to try to squeeze into the "skinny jeans" that no longer fit, I offer the same advice for choosing a career. Don't try to be someone you're not. Keep looking for the right fit until you find it.

Feed your subconscious mind
Believe in the power of your subconscious to know what is best for you. It is always turned on and available to help, even while you sleep. Choose to tap into it for assistance. Evidence of this

Work On Your Own Terms

power comes in the form of intuition, hunches, and gut feelings. You can feed a problem to your subconscious, and the solution may appear to you in a dream. Artists, musicians, scientists, and writers all tap into this vault for inspiration. Follow their example.

The Power of Thirty Days
It takes between twenty-one and thirty days to form a new habit. *Work on Your Own Terms* has thirty chapters with suggestions and exercises at the end of each one (not including the introductory chapter). You might want to read the book through once and then take thirty days to re-read one chapter each day. Explore the suggestions and complete the exercises each day. The habit you are working on is rewiring your brain to view the world through a different lens so you can create life on your own terms.

The Legend of the Hundredth Monkey
If you have never read *The Hundredth Monkey* by Ken Keyes, Jr., you owe it to yourself to do so. His book is deliberately not copyrighted, so anyone can access it. It is "dedicated to the Dinosaurs, who mutely warn us that a species which cannot adapt to changing conditions will become extinct."

The main theme of Keye's book is preventing nuclear war. The sub-theme is the one this book addresses—how our consciousness, creativity, and way of thinking can change our lives and our world for the better. I first quoted from this book twelve years ago when I wrote my thesis on *The Future of Work*. What I'm seeing now is the "hundredth monkey" in action. Let me explain.

This is the Legend
In 1952, on the Japanese island of Koshima, scientists were providing monkeys with sweet potatoes dropped in the sand. The monkeys liked the taste of the potatoes, but found the dirt unpleasant. Eventually, one of the young monkeys started washing her potatoes in a stream. She taught this to her mother and playmates who taught this to their mothers. Between 1952 and 1958, all the young monkeys had learned to wash the potatoes prior to eating. Only the adults who imitated their children learned this. Other adults kept eating dirty potatoes.

Overview - What's It All About?

11

In the autumn of 1958, a certain number of monkeys were washing potatoes. The number was guessed to be ninety-nine. Then the one hundredth monkey started washing her potatoes. A tipping point had been reached. By that evening, almost everyone in the tribe started washing their potatoes. This one hundredth monkey had created an idealogical breakthrough.

What was even more surprising, though, was somehow the potato washing jumped over the sea. Colonies of mainland monkeys began washing their potatoes. This new awareness had been communicated invisibly from mind-to-mind (*without the help of the Internet*). This leads me to wonder: Is there a point at which a critical mass of people will also gain access to a new awareness?

Will you be the Hundredth Monkey?
Do you believe in synchronicity? I experienced it a lot while writing this book. It seemed as if every thought I had, or book I read, kept leading me to someone else who thought with a similar mindset. Are we close to revolutionizing the way we all live and work?

Ken Keyes asked: "Will you accept your share of the responsibility for creating the Hundredth Monkey energy that will change the consciousness of the entire planet? . . . Begin doing things now that are so desperately needed for the conscious unfolding of your life—and the survival of our species . . . You will begin to discover the miracle of your full potential as a human being. Your life will gain meaning and purpose . . . The Hundredth Monkey Phenomenon points out our responsibility and our power."

Are we now close to the tipping point to a better future of work? If you are thinking you need to make a change—don't wait too long before you act. Don't allow someone else to control your present or your future.

No more begging for jobs
Begging for jobs in the manner of a typical job search is often a blow to your self-esteem. Sending out oodles of resumes, cover

letters and smiling through interviews rarely result in the job of your dreams. After working as a career counsellor and teaching these skills for many years, I recognized there must be a better way.

Job search is often like trying to fit a square peg into a round hole. Think of yourself as a puzzle piece you are trying to squeeze into a square or round hole, and you will recognize that parts of you will need to be shaved off.

While none of us can control the global economy, each of us can determine our own destiny, economic condition, and happiness. The world is telling us we need to live differently. Don't allow fear to stop you. Face your fears and take steps to overcome them. Future work requires being open to new ideas, taking educated risks, experimentation, an appetite for innovation, and a willingness to collaborate with others. We are all writing the story of our lives. Express yourself and hear your own voice and create a work/life that fits your own shape. Recognize that you have the power to create your own opportunities.

About the soundtrack for this book
Artists and musicians can often articulate our feelings in a way we can relate to, but are unable to express ourselves. Music can touch us in a way no other art form does.

Although I find it too distracting to listen to music while I'm writing, a number of song lyrics danced in my head during the process of completing this book. I've interwoven them into the chapters and suggest you have a listen to them on YouTube. Remember K-tel records? They were compilation music albums that were extensively advertised on TV when I was a kid. The songs visit a number of musical genres and reflect an eclectic taste in music. It's a trip down memory lane for most of us.

You might want to download the songs from iTunes to create your own modern version of a K-tel record as the soundtrack to this book. Let me know if this music speaks to you.

Put fear on a balloon and release it
I've experienced all six of the fears Napoleon Hill identified (poverty, criticism, poor health, loss of love, old age, and death). Once you are aware of your limiting beliefs, you will be able to make a conscious decision to overcome them.

It has been said that fear is man's greatest enemy. Fear can cause failure if it stops you from walking through it. However, fear is only a thought in your mind. Don't fear your own thoughts. Change them if they are not helping you get what you want. The only fears that were not given to us by others are the fear of falling and the fear of loud noises. All other fears have been taught to us. Refuse to accept their lessons. Stay focused on what you want.

We need to break free of the self-imposed prison we have unwittingly placed ourselves in due to our beliefs, opinions, training, and environmental influences. We have been conditioned to react as we do —like Pavlov's dog who salivated for his dinner every time a bell was rung. We fall into our habits and will stay there unless we deliberately change them. To live and work on your own terms, you need to generate the feelings and emotions you associate with having that freedom before it will manifest in reality.

Create meaning amidst chaos
Who better to look to for advice on how to create meaning amidst chaos than Viktor Frankl, who was held for years in dehumanizing concentration camps: "Personal restlessness and concern about individual security are pushing many people to ask fresh questions about their working lives, but world events are also something of a wake-up call . . . security has economic, social and environmental dimensions . . . the only way any one of us can be secure is if we are all secure." He stressed our need to understand the "why" of our existence.

Without exception, all of the people I interviewed in depth for *The Future of Work* revealed they had made conscious choices about what to do with their lives based on taking time to examine their own needs, dreams, and desires.

Ask yourself what you're looking for. Where do you want your life to take you? One of the messages from *Alice in Wonderland* is this: "If you don't know where you're going, any road will take you there." *Work On Your Own Terms* will help you decide where you want to go and how to get there.

Our beliefs create our reality
Which statement sounds more true to you?

I'll believe it when I see it.
OR
I'll see it when I believe it.

Both are true. Your reality rests in the statement you believe.

If family and friends start telling you to play it safe and to stay with the job you have, even though you feel you have outgrown it, don't listen. If people tell you you're a dreamer, thank them, and let them know that everything new begins in the imagination. It was Albert Einstein who said, "Imagination is more important than knowledge." It starts with a dream and progresses with action. I hope you'll travel this road with me.

I cannot specify what gift of soul to you will be at midlife. I can only suggest that when it is presented, it be received.

Murray Stein

Record your thoughts as you read through each chapter. We'll be putting together the puzzle pieces of the life you envision. By the last chapter, you will have a full picture of both why and how you want to work on your own terms. Move into the next phase of your life with intent, purpose, and following the lifestyle of your dreams.

Chapter 2:
Create Your Own Destiny

The questions you ask on a daily basis will shape your destiny as clearly as the skeleton shapes your body.

Martin Luther King, Jr.

Keep your mind open to change all the time. Welcome it. Court it. It is only by examining and re-examining your opinions and ideas that you can progress.

Dale Carnegie

Let's start by looking at our belief system.

It begins in childhood. A parent's attitude and beliefs often shape the attitude and performance of their children. If your parents believed you would never learn to tie your shoes—you might only be wearing slip-ons or Velcro fasteners today.

In the mid-80s, I worked as a Life Skills Coach for teens with a variety of mental and physical disabilities who led sheltered lives because their parents thought they were helping them by enabling them to be largely dependent on others. Recognizing this, we created a live-in camp to teach them basic life skills. By the end of the summer, great progress had been made and most of the participants were able to make a simple meal, successfully navigate their way on transit and had completed mock job interviews with the staff.

Over the past few years, I have shown job seekers a YouTube video of motivational speaker, Nick Vujicic, who was born without arms or legs. When he was a baby, his father taught him how to swim. Today, he not only works for a living, but he can write, golf, play drums, surf, fish, dive and perform numerous other activities. His motto is "Life without limbs, but no limits."

Vujicic says: "What do you want? You have to visualize yourself overcoming any obstacles." (*Google "Nick Vujicic – Life without limits" to see for yourself.*)

When was the last time you examined your beliefs? Are your beliefs moving you forward or holding you back? Are they your beliefs or were they passed on to you by someone else?

Possible thoughts you might have had:
I'm too old to change careers.
It's too hard to retrain.
I'll never be able to earn a good living.
I don't have the time or money to do what I want.
That's easy for you to say, but . . .

If you believe you are too old to change careers, this belief is unlikely to motivate you to make a career change because you believe the effort would be fruitless. Limiting beliefs can prevent you from reaching your potential. When thoughts are partnered with emotional intensity, beliefs become ingrained. Whenever you are under stress and revert to childlike behaviour, you are likely re-experiencing a belief formed in childhood.

I remember in grade school standing to give a speech I had memorized, and my mind went completely blank. I couldn't remember a single word. I was forced to stand there while the teacher and entire class laughed at me. Even today, after working as a workshop facilitator for many years, I am still not comfortable with public speaking in front of large groups. We all know that we can't get out of an anxious situation by looking away. We have to find a way to walk through it.

Since at least the time of Socrates, we have been advised to "know thyself," and told that "the unexamined life is not worth living." Examine your thoughts to see what you believe and decide if any changes are needed to make your life more worth living. Our beliefs are the stories we tell ourselves, either consciously or subconsciously. We can create self-fulfilling prophecies around a false belief we have about ourselves.

When you hear of people who have won a large sum of money in a lottery and then go broke shortly afterwards, could the cause be that they are still living with a "poverty mentality" or, are they just "unlucky"?

Others with a "wealth mentality" can lose everything, go broke, and then regain wealth within a short time. Do you believe it's because they are just "lucky"?

When Oprah tells us the reason a poor, black, abused child was able to rise to great wealth and prominence was that she always believed she was destined for greatness, is there a clue for us in her words?

Quantum Physics demystified
You are probably familiar with the New Age phrase: Our thoughts create our reality. Now science, specifically, quantum physics, has proven a connection between the mind and physical matter.

Quantum physics is the study of the behaviour of matter and energy at the subatomic level. It implies that our thoughts can affect the behaviour of subatomic particles.

Science has demonstrated that our observation of reality changes reality. We are always consciously or unconsciously in the process of creating what we experience in our lives. When we understand this, we realize that others cannot control us without our permission. We can control our own thoughts and behaviours. Everything is energy. Thoughts are energy. We are vibrational beings living in a vibrational universe. Thought is the most potent form of energy and it can now be measured.

To see evidence of this, you can Google photos of the experiments of Masaru Emoto in which he played various types of music and sent either positive or negative thoughts to vials of distilled water, which were then frozen and the crystalline structures studied. The results were amazing. Each emotion relayed to the water vials resulted in different patterns in the crystals when viewed under a microscope. Positive emotions produced much more beautiful and complex designs than did negative emotions. Keep in mind that most of your body is composed of water. What messages are you sending to the water molecules in your own body—or the bodies of those around you? What effect is that producing?

To construct our ideal work life, we need to harness the most powerful force in the universe—our beliefs. When we focus on our limitations, we attract more limitations. When we focus on our desires, we attract more of what we desire. This is the message in the movie *The Secret*.

We often live lives that prevent us from seeing things as they could be. The problem is that many of us spend most of our lives on autopilot. Have you ever driven home from work and not really remembered doing so when you arrived?

Before deciding on a new career path, we need to become aware of any self-limiting beliefs we have, so we can change them. Let's take a further look at how our brains operate.

Bruce Lipton, PhD, is a stem cell biologist and the author of *Biology of Belief and Spontaneous Evolution*. His work bridges science and spirit. His research shows that we are not victims of our genes, and that our genes are merely blueprints. As when building a house, the blueprints can be changed. He says we are like contractors who can construct our own lives by the way we use our minds.

We have the power to change our minds by changing our beliefs. Some of our beliefs may have been set before we learned how to speak. Therefore, it requires a conscious effort to change a belief that doesn't serve us.

Dr. Lipton asserts that placing genetically identical cells in different environments changes the fate of the cells. In view of this, he suggests we choose an environment that nurtures and supports us in developing our potential, as we are composed of innumerable cells that can be influenced and altered by our surroundings. As evidence, he maintains children adopted into families prone to cancer or heart disease can develop those conditions even though their genetics don't carry that tendency. He argues that we have the power to change our perceptions and beliefs, and that our minds' perception of the world can change our biology.

Does our programming need an upgrade?
What has brought us to our current place in life is our past programming at an unconscious level. This programming has been absorbed during our childhood and later—through our families, peers, teachers, media, and culture. Some of us never question our beliefs or where they came from. The same computer programs keep repeating in our brain. It may be time for an upgrade.

We can learn from each new experience. We don't need to repeat it. Unlike in the movie *Groundhog Day*, we don't need to keep reliving the same thing over and over again. Once you've learned the lesson, move on to something new. If something isn't working, try a different approach.

In the '80s, I was a Katimavik group leader working with youths from across Canada who were doing volunteer work in local communities. A participant in the town next to mine told her group leader that her head hurt from being forced to think for herself. At age nineteen, it was something she had never done before. I found this somewhat alarming—given that she was able to get a driver's license at age sixteen—but encouraged that she was actually starting to think more deeply.

The BBC documentary, *Seven Up*, is based on the premise: "Give me a child until he is seven, and I will give you the man." The program re-filmed participants every seven years to see if this was true. You can view episodes on YouTube.

The good news is we can re-program ourselves at any age. An easy way to do this is to ask yourself, after every decision you make, why you chose the way you did. Keep asking why until you get to the root of your answer. Question your old programming so you don't live your life on autopilot.

It's hard to fight the system while you're in it
If you feel held back by bureaucracy and hierarchy, you will need to leave that system. There is no need to give power to someone or something you disagree with. Simply carve your own path. Follow the advice given by Mahatma Gandhi and "be the change you wish to see in the world."

Think about how often you choose different ways of behaving with family members than with friends or co-workers. Think about the daily choices you make. Whenever you make an automatic or unconscious choice, it is likely that someone from your past has chosen for you. Since our beliefs are unconscious habits, we can dig them up and consciously change them if we aren't getting what we want in our lives. This could be the key to designing and achieving a fulfilling life.

If you want to know what choices you've made in the past and whether or not they have served you well, look at your life up to the present. It will reflect the choices you've made. When you make better choices, your life changes for the better. We are the sum of all the choices we make in life. Choose consciously.

Bees do it. So can we
Scientists at Arizona State University have discovered that older foraging honeybees are able to reverse brain aging when

younger bees responsible for the larvae (bee babies) have been removed from a hive. The older bees learned how to care for the larvae and within ten days, about 50 percent of them had significantly improved their ability to learn new things. Scientists also discovered a change in the proteins in the bees' brains. It is the same proteins that are being studied to treat age-related dementia in people. If an old bee can learn new things, so can we (Baker et al., 2012).

Visualize what you want
Since it's been shown that your brain cannot distinguish reality from imagination, the saying "Fake it until you make it" is good advice in terms of reprogramming negative beliefs into positive ones. Keep in mind that it often takes twenty-one to thirty days of consistent practice to create your new habit or belief.

Because your mind sees the world as pictures rather than words, a Vision Board can be a useful tool to help focus on your desires. This may appeal to you more than writing out the exercises at the end of each chapter. You can create a Vision Board for yourself by cutting out images of what you would like in your life and pasting them onto a board for daily review. (*You may want to place your Vision Board in a picture frame so it's a bit more attractive. Include pictures that represent some of the emotions you would like to experience more of—joy, love, etc.*)

Olympic athletes often use visualization to enhance their performance. You can use this concept by visualizing yourself (in your imagination) going through all the steps you need to take to enable yourself to work on your own terms.

Remember to take at least one small step every day for thirty days, and you will create a new habit. Read one chapter a day to help your rewiring process. While visualizing each step, engage the aid of all your senses. With the addition of strong positive emotions, you can create a "positive memory" of yourself in action, in your imagination. (*This is the "Fake it until you make it" advice.*)

Keep in mind these Three Powerful Success Principles:

1. Decide what you want, and why you want it.
   Write it on a card you can carry with you.
   Read it daily.
2. Believe you can achieve it.
3. Take Action Steps to make your dream reality.

Revisit all three steps daily until your goal is attained.

Reminder: Read a chapter a day for thirty days.

Complete the exercises at the end of each chapter.

Repeat this process until you are living and working on your own terms.
Test for yourself the theory that twenty-one to thirty days of practice will create a new habit that leads you toward your chosen future. The new habit is to daily rewire your brain to support your belief about your ability to work on your own terms. This is what a new musician must do to learn to play a musical instrument. We need to rewire our brain circuits until they become automatic and support us in playing our own tune. (*I started playing the ukulele just as I began writing this book.*)

Be open to different perspectives
Anais Nin said: "We don't see things as they are, but as we are." We are often so caught up in the busyness of living that we don't allow ourselves time for reflection and to question our perspectives. When we can see things differently, we may choose to act differently. This is how people discovered the world was not flat—although I've heard some still believe it is.

Edward de Bono founded the Centre for the Study of Thinking and created a curriculum to teach thinking in schools and business. In his book, *Future Positive*, he emphasized the need to broaden our perceptions and develop positive thinking habits— for as he says, our perspective on life determines the future we end up living. Think about how your perspective can be used to create the future you desire.

We cannot solve our current global problems through old ways of thinking. We need to practice thinking differently by tapping into our own innate creativity. This book presents a number of different perspectives for you to consider. Think about them and choose elements you'd like to carry into your own future. Consciously choose the ones you believe will make you happy.

De Bono suggested we embrace the benefits technology can provide to create a better future for ourselves. He proposed we use it to "give us the time and freedom to escape from the tyranny of mere survival."

This really is no time for apathy. Individually, we can create a positive future for ourselves through our attitude and our thinking habits. Collectively, that will create a positive future for all of us.

Soundtrack 🎵

The lyrics that keep playing in my head are from the old Beatles song, "Revolution":

You say you want a revolution.
Well, you know, we all want to change the world.

My response is—*Revolution for One, please.*

Revolution for One
I hope you will start your own *Revolution for One*. As corporations continue to downsize, we must realize that we are all in business for ourselves—whether we have a job with an employer, or we are entrepreneurs. See yourself as a micro-business and decide which products or services are your best match. Regardless of how we choose to work, we are renting our time and talent out to others. Become conscious of the unique value you bring to the world.

Forget the old economy job search

There is work available for everyone who wants to work—but it is not neatly packaged in a job description. It's really the work you create for yourself after looking within. As with building a house, you will need to decide on a number of things before you can even lay the foundation. Where do you want to build? In designing your own work, the first question is where do you want to live and work? What's your ideal environment? Thanks to technology, information work is portable.

What follows are your design needs. How many rooms do you want? One storey or two? In work search, the building blocks are your values, needs, skills, and goals. Most job searches show you the finished product first (Job Description) and teach you how to lay the bricks (Resumé and Cover Letter), before you have built your foundation. That's why many jobs fall apart. It's because they are built on shaky ground. You need a solid base on which to build your ideal life, which includes your ideal work.

Old economy job searches no longer work and are less than fulfilling for midlife career changers. Our midlife work must feed both our body and soul. People who are self-motivated and passionate about their work don't need to be managed by someone else. In midlife, we just need to discover the work we would love to do—and then just do it!

When I first began working as a career counsellor, I was able to facilitate a one-week career exploration program. Although even that was a short time-frame, clients enjoyed it as a first step to get them thinking about who they were and what they were seeking in their work. As the funding for that program eroded, my job title changed to employment advisor, with a focus on getting clients a job as quickly as possible. It was less important for the work to be a good match. It didn't take long for me to reclaim my path as a career counsellor.

What you stand for

Before you reject any ideas in this book, I invite you to play with them in your mind. See which elements might have merit in your own life. Then, tap into your creativity to evolve and customize these ideas for yourself. Often my words are meant to provoke you to both think and act in a different way. They are not meant to tell you what to do. There is no one-size-fits-all, although pantyhose manufacturers might have sold us that myth.

It is usually easy for us to protest and know what we are against. The challenge is to know what we stand for. By the time we've reached midlife, most of us realize we are not here just to make a living, but to make a difference.

To live life on your own terms requires self-awareness and a willingness to take risks that might separate you from your peers. Others will try to plant their own fears into you, if you let them. Fear is a way to manipulate and control people. It's part of our culture. It's often part of our family heritage, and it is often used in a workplace based on hierarchy. I'm convinced that's why many people stay in a workplace that doesn't feed their souls. It's what they know. (*Can you recall the saying: Better the devil you know than the one you don't?*) When you grow up with dysfunction, and your workplace is also dysfunctional—it feels like a natural fit. It isn't. Decide to make your escape.

I believe we live in a time of unprecedented opportunity, and the world really is "our oyster." The challenge is we need to be willing to pry open our shell and look around.

Don't wait for government and institutions to change
Large institutions that operate under a hierarchy or bureaucracy are not about to change. The system serves maintaining the status quo. It is much easier for us as individuals to change than it is for an institution. Who can turn on a dime? An elephant or a mouse?

Don't allow fear to control you
An awful lot of our media and advertising is based on fear-based marketing. *Buy a new car so you don't look like a loser. Buy this deodorant so friends won't shun you. The unemployment rate is so high it's unlikely you will ever work again.* That kind of

nonsense is meant to dull us into buying whatever they are selling—usually it's paranoia. Fear is a way to control people.

What is under-reported is the growing movement toward social enterprise and the incredible amount of good work happening in the world. You might want to turn off commercial TV and watch some public television or listen to TED talks or search for webinars on a favourite topic. There is a lot of good information available if you choose to look for it.

Often, we have so many people telling us what we can't do that we start to believe it—the self-fulfilling prophecy. Let's break that mold together.

At the end of each chapter, I pose a few questions. It's important for you to decide for yourself what you want, who you want to be, and how you will live and work. Give that message to your subconscious mind on a consistent basis. It will lead to ultimate fulfillment.

This book is intentionally designed to provoke you to think differently – to create a *Revolution for One*. By changing your world and creating a positive future for yourself, others will follow. In the past, I've been accused of being a bit of a rabble-rouser, although I like to think of it as a catalyst for change. Now that I'm almost sixty, I think it is time for me to fully embrace who I am. Isn't this what Abraham Maslow taught us? To live fully we need to embrace and use our gifts to self-actualize. I invite you to join me.

Why people remain unemployed
Everyone who wants to work, deserves to work. The biggest reason that people remain unemployed is that they are not clear about how they can best use their gifts to serve the world. Your work needs to reflect your core values and utilize your favourite gifts/skills to provide a product or service you believe benefits others. If you are out of alignment in any of these, your work will not fulfill you. All three work together.

Core		Favourite		Benefits		
Values	+	Gifts/Skills	+	Others	=	Your Dream Work

The next step is to set your Intention to manifest your dream work into reality. Notice the synchronicities that will start to manifest. Who are the people and what are the events that come into your life to nudge you to grow? Sometimes we come across people who mirror an aspect of ourselves we need to work on. Every challenge carries a seed of opportunity with it. Whenever you find yourself in an uncomfortable situation, ask yourself what you can learn from it.

What did Edgar Cayce know?
Edgar Cayce was a deeply religious man and a well-known medium/psychic who spoke of the power of our subconscious mind long before the discovery of brain plasticity and the movie, *The Secret*, was produced.

While in trance, Cayce stated, "The subconscious mind forgets nothing . . . a man becomes what he feeds into his subconscious" (Cayce, 1964). We can observe the power of suggestion on the physical body by the behaviour of people under hypnosis. Have you ever seen a hypnotist on stage with volunteers from the audience when he feeds the suggestion that ants are crawling all over their bodies or it's so cold in the room that they must be shivering—and the volunteers act this out? This is the power of suggestion in action.

Cayce was one of the first people to speak about the Law of Attraction. He repeatedly stressed that our minds create our reality and that positive thoughts and actions are essential for genuine self-expression. He explained our need to "be of service, have integrity, self-discipline, and to always ask: What are my motives? What is my purpose?"

He believed a person could use meditation or prayer to open doors to resources within himself that would enable him to better serve his fellow man. He also said one of the greatest obstacles man must cope with is fear. Once we start to take action to move toward our dreams, resistance often sets in. Thoughts and feelings we'd rather not face will surface. Stay focused on what you want and walk through them.

Cayce thought fear to be the greatest destructive force to man's intelligence and the root of most of the ills of mankind. He suggested, for example, the best way to overcome the fear of advancing old age or being alone is to go out and do something for somebody else. He said above all, we are here to serve others.

Sue Frederick, author of *I See Your Dream Job*, claims that our most rewarding work will likely arise out of our desire to show people how we've overcome our own fears or personal hurdles. In doing so, we share with others how they can do the same. When our work conforms to our mission, she points out, we cannot help but prosper.

Action Steps – Questions to Ponder

Would you live differently if you knew you could utilize much more of your potential by developing the habit of making more conscious choices?

Are you committed to living and working on your own terms?

Soundtrack ♪

Bob Marley was singing his "Redemption Song" in my head at the end of this chapter. Here are a couple of lines:

Emancipate yourselves from mental slavery;
none but ourselves can free our minds.

Books You Might Like to Read

Biology of Belief
by Bruce Lipton, PhD

Spontaneous Evolution
by Bruce Lipton, PhD

Future Positive
by Edward de Bono

Venture Inward (about Edgar Cayce)
by Hugh Lynn Cayce (his son)

I See Your Dream Job
by Sue Frederick

Also Google

www.lumosity.com

This site offers a series of brain games to make your brain smarter.
They are based on the principle of neuroplasticity.

I.

FEAR OF POVERTY

Chapter 3:
The Economics Of Freedom

The price of anything is the amount of life you exchange for it.

Henry David Thoreau

The lack of money is the number one fear that trips up most of us. I've lost track of the number of women who have said they are afraid of becoming bag ladies. Part of the problem with any discussion of money is the fact that people are often defined by their net worth. We also struggle with the question of who is richer—she who has more time or she who has more money?

Which role model do you admire more? Mother Theresa or Donald Trump? Have they both lived their lives on purpose? Is it really money that is the measure of our success? I will assume you need some kind of income. You will decide how much is enough.

Napoleon Hill said: "If you want riches (on a financial, material, mental or spiritual level), you must first refuse to accept any circumstance that leads toward poverty. The starting point of the path that leads to riches is desire."

Refuse to accept a poverty mindset. This mentality will destroy your enthusiasm, self-reliance, imagination, and initiative and replace it with procrastination, lack of ambition, and uncertainty of purpose. Decide not to fall into this trap! Focus on wealth creation instead. If that term sends shudders down your spine, it may indicate ambiguous feelings about money.

Hill claimed the reason he wrote a book about money was that "so many people are paralyzed by the fear of poverty." Although we can't measure riches in dollars alone, he said people told him: "Give me all the money I need, and I will find everything else I want."

Look for great ideas
What creates money is ideas. Every product or service you have used began as an idea. The best products and services serve a need. Many of us become disillusioned with our jobs when we don't believe our work is serving a genuine need.

What need does your work serve?
Let's explore how our work can serve our needs. A job isn't necessary to earn a living. The economists of freedom suggest we examine all of our options. Money is merely a by-product of humanity. It does not make the world go 'round.

Get clear about your personal values—based on how you prefer to spend your time and money. We are always spending one or the other. This will help you determine the amount of income you'll need and how many hours a week you will need to work in which to earn it. The greater number of needs you have, the more you'll need to earn—especially if what you crave are luxuries you don't really need.

What pulls us forward is a definite purpose in life. Find a cause you believe in and work for it. It is often something you wish to learn that gives a clue to your personal mission. You can then use your skills to market a meaningful product or service that will provide your income.

The price of freedom
Freedom poses a difficult choice for many of us. If you truly want to work on your own terms, it often necessitates relinquishing a regular paycheque. If you lack initiative and self-discipline, a manager who tells you what to do and when may be just what you need. Either choice has a cost. How much freedom can you truly handle? Good self-knowledge is essential before you take the leap.

In-depth interviews with Boomers who had transitioned from a job to self-employment reveal a list of pros and cons for each choice. Although none of those interviewed wished to reverse their decision, they all knew the price they had paid to move on.

Action Steps

Read each list and place a check mark beside the items you need to have in your life. The list with the most check marks will indicate the type of employment you should probably be seeking.

Regular job pros
- steady paycheque
- paid vacation
- paid sick leave
- health-care coverage
- co-workers to socialize with
- no need to look for work
- professional development days

Self-employment pros
- greater freedom and autonomy
- freedom to grow / self-development
- work hours more flexible
- no age limit
- no office politics
- work aligned with values
- ability to balance work and personal life
- earning potential without ceiling
- opportunity to use creativity and fulfill potential
- opportunity to form strategic partnerships
- ability to fulfill desire to give back
- better tax breaks

Also consider the drawbacks:

Regular job cons
- job duties and hours of work controlled by others
- office politics

- hierarchy and bureaucracy
- little opportunity for creativity
- little incentive to show initiative
- not enough flexibility
- rules made by others
- job insecurity

Self-employment cons
- unpredictable income
- need to pay for own benefits
- greater administrative burden
- need to be self-disciplined
- need to budget for lean times
- need to finance one's own professional development
- regular self-marketing required

If you favour some items from each choice, you may want to combine a part-time job with part-time self-employment. It is safer to have more than one source of income.

Do you prefer a regular job, self-employment, or a mix of the two?

The fear of poverty may be the biggest fear you will need to address. Let's look at the Voluntary Simplicity movement in the following chapter for assistance.

Chapter 4:
How Much Is Enough?

We must realize that when basic needs have been met, human development is primarily about being more, not having more.

The Dalai Lama

The biggest secret of the "Voluntary Simplicity" movement is that you can live comfortably with less than you thought possible. Our economy depends heavily on continuous consumption of goods and services—the very thing that may destroy our planet. Surely, we can choose a different way to live.

When people experience a natural disaster and lose everything, they often re-evaluate their lives. I spoke with a woman who lost both her home and home-based business in a fire. She and her family were safe. She also managed to save her computer hard drive and some personal belongings including family photos. She said that although the initial effect was devastating, it actually felt very freeing to have lost the rest of her possessions. Imagine how a similar situation might help you reassess your own life.

Does this story sound familiar to you?
You may have heard the parable of the businessman and the fisherman already. It's been around for decades. There are several versions of it easily found on the Internet. No one seems to know who wrote the original. The following is the story I'm most familiar with.

A businessman on vacation in Mexico sees a fisherman pull up to the dock with several large fish in his boat. He asks the fisherman how long it took him to catch the fish. The fisherman says it only took him a few hours and adds that his catch is more than enough to support his family. The businessman sees that the fisherman is missing out on a great opportunity and tries to convince him to upscale his business.

The fisherman describes how he spends the rest of the day with his wife and children, and in the evening strolls into the village to have a sip of wine where he sings and plays music with his friends. The businessman tries to talk him into fishing longer each day, buying a bigger boat, and eventually a whole fleet. He tells the fisherman that after that, he could open his own cannery and move to a city where he could further expand his business. He estimates the whole process shouldn't take more than twenty years, after which the fisherman would be a very rich man.

When the fisherman asks him what he should do with all that money, the businessman tells him he could then retire, move to a quaint fishing village, spend more time with his wife and grandchildren and stroll into the village in the evening to have a sip of wine and sing and play music with his friends.

Know what really matters in life, and you may find that it is already much closer than you think. In fact, I live on a small island, and the lifestyle the fisherman describes is very similar to the life of many of my fellow islanders.

It may surprise you to learn that billionaire Warren Buffet still lives in the same neighbourhood he grew up in and associates with the same people he did in high school. Even after making millions, he kept driving an old Volkswagen Beetle. He believes children who inherit great wealth tend to do nothing with their lives. For this reason, he donated thirty-two billion dollars to charity. Buffet defines success as "being loved by the people you hope love you. You can be the richest man in the world, but without the love of family and friends, you would also be the poorest." It sounds as if his family had no objection to his giving the money away.

A lack of critical thinking skills can lead to peer pressure and an attitude of keeping up with the Joneses that advertisers love. Real estate agents are surprised at the number of retirees who are now buying monster "dream homes." My personal vision of future housing in these homes is along the lines of the TV show, *The Golden Girls.* This is likely to become a more popular way of living in the future as Boomers often lived communally in their youth.

Two of my single friends approached retirement from opposite ends of the spectrum. One is retiring at age sixty with the government pension program he has paid into but with no employer pension. He chose not to buy a house but to rent a one-bedroom apartment in a small city near the ocean. His maximum earnings have always been less than $50,000 per year. He has saved a percentage of his income on a regular basis and will start to draw on his savings next year, if he needs to. His needs are simple and he is sure his pension will cover most of them.

The other friend is now aged sixty-six. She is already qualified to collect a full government pension and will also qualify for a healthy pension from her employer should she choose to retire. However, she is afraid to. Her financial planner has told her she needs to have at least one million dollars in the bank before she can even consider retiring. Really? I wonder how much that fellow is making in commission? She continues to work full-time. Although she enjoys her work most of the time, she has little free time for her hobbies.

Which scenario more likely describes you?

Hollywood is full of stories about how money and material possessions have not delivered the happiness expected. We might keep hearing that continuous consumer spending is the way to make the economy grow, but at what cost to the individual? Work holds a negative connotation if you are working just to pay the bills. The biggest challenge many of us have is the difficulty of maintaining our focus on what we truly want to do because of the multitude of distractions coming at us on a daily basis. Pro-actively choosing simplicity is a way to regain control over your life so you can then move forward at your own pace.

I recently heard a budding photographer, Anne McKinnell, talk about what launched her off in a new direction. She sold her city home and traded in her full-time job for life on the road in an RV. She felt she had been living in a world of darkness and negativity which was pulling her down. She made a conscious decision to use photography as a way to focus only on the good things she saw. It allowed her to alter her perspective on how she viewed the world. A friend had asked her: "If you knew you could not fail, what would you do or be?" She pulled out her Bucket List and noticed travel across Canada and the United States was on it. She is now living her life story, not just dreaming about it, and is also a whole lot happier.

This is the third person I've met who has chosen this route. The other two were single women who also sold their homes and moved full-time into an RV from which each works on the road. I've met others who live and work from their boat. This appears to be a growing trend. People are increasingly making the decision to move to a location that provides the lifestyle they want and then figuring out the work that matches that location. I recommend you plan the two simultaneously.

I credit backpacking through Europe in my twenties for opening my eyes to the joys of simplicity. Not only did I carry on my back most of what I needed for a year, I also spoke with people in the Greek islands who although poor by North American standards, were happier by far than those I had left behind. At that time, I had no phone, no Internet connection, no TV or portable sound system. Instead, I attended live music events, mingled with the locals, and lived communally. This showed me that all I really need is my own room with access to a bathroom, kitchen, and living space.

A few years ago, I was totally shocked when I walked into a local retail store. As I walked up and down the aisles, all I saw was a host of cheap plastic products. Some items might have been useful, but they looked as if they would easily break. The rest looked like useless junk. I was taken aback by the waste of good resources to bring these products to market when they were destined for the garbage dump in less than one generation.

When the West Edmonton Mall first opened, I read that people from England were flying over for a one-week vacation to stay on-site at a hotel in the mall and shopping under glass the whole time they were there. Is that not a sad way to visit a foreign country?

I'm sure the Mall was not serenading shoppers with one of my favourite Bluegrass Gospel tunes: *You can't take it with you when you go*. The best line is "You'll never see a U-haul pulled behind a hearse."

Unfortunately, Canadians are retiring with significant amounts of debt. According to Statistics Canada, about two-thirds of workers age fifty-five plus now have some form of debt in the form of a mortgage, line of credit or a credit card balance that is carried forward from month-to-month (CBC News, 2011; Marshall, 2012). Boomers are being blamed for lack of foresight to invest in retirement savings plans at the same time economists are telling us it is increased consumer spending that will save the economy, and advertisers keep screaming "Buy, Buy, Buy." It's not surprising people are confused.

Best advice on how to reclaim your money savvy
Figure out how much money you actually need to bring in each month in order to feel secure in your ability to cover expenses. Read *Your Money or Your Life* by Joe Dominguez and Vicki Robin and complete the exercises suggested. The authors emphasize everything we buy is traded for a percentage of our life energy. Are you spending your energy wisely? You may learn you can live on much less than you anticipated. If you can lower your expenses and work part-time, it will free you to explore other options. Almost anything is too costly if it holds you back from realizing your potential.

Consider downsizing your living arrangement. Can you move to a smaller-scale home in a less-costly neighbourhood? Eliminate all the clutter in your life. Inventory all the items you own that you neither like nor use. Sell or give them away. They not only take up physical space, but may also take up emotional space—in the form of regret. It may help to view this as a temporary measure that will give you the breathing space you need to design your future lifestyle.

Before you spend, determine what each item will cost in terms of your life energy. For example, if it takes you ten hours to make one hundred dollars net, and you buy yourself a one hundred dollar sweater, is that a good return on your investment of time and energy? Hopefully, it won't end up in the back of a closet, never to be worn.

Simply by becoming more conscious of your spending habits, you may be able to rebuild your life more economically than you believed possible. Start by dividing your purchases into those that bring you pleasure and those that leave you feeling guilt or regret. Eliminate those purchases you'll soon regret. Pay special attention to the relationship between spending and stress. Retail therapy is usually unconscious spending that does not address the core issue. It was Mother Theresa who said "sometimes people can hunger for more than bread." Overconsumption is often related to stress.

Clutter and excessive busyness can distract us from focusing on what is truly important. Think of money as a form of energy. Sometimes we give it the power to free us. Often it binds us to it. Money exists to serve—not to dominate our existence. It is simply a medium of exchange with no intrinsic value. We don't need money as much as we need to have something we can trade for other things we can't produce ourselves.

If you are already retired and your income can cover your basic needs, you might want a part-time job or self-employment to satisfy your wants. Choose something you find personally rewarding and enjoyable, so it combines both work and play. In fact, if you can't distinguish work from your play, you won't need to consider retiring. How many retired artists have you heard of?

Choose to invest in yourself. It is one of the most important decisions you will make in your life. Invest in what you need to feel good on the inside. This will help curb buying things you don't need. The less stress each individual has, the less stress there is spilling out into the rest of the world.

Even if you are not familiar with the work of Abraham Maslow, you will realize that you need to satisfy your basic needs for food, water, shelter and companionship before you can move toward self-actualizing your higher goals. This is the gift of Voluntary Simplicity. It enables you to satisfy the basics so you can then concentrate on your higher goals. It was a wise man who said those with the fewest needs are the richest.

No one likes to head out the door singing: "I owe, I owe, so off to work I go." Don't be like one of my husband's former co-workers. He retired at sixty with his mortgage paid off and money in the bank. He and his wife then decided they needed a boat as well as a much larger home that came with a mortgage. He went back to work full-time at age sixty-three. He said it was because he needed more toys. Do you need more toys? Will you have time to play with them?

Don't think of this as a permanent way to live—just as a transition phase. You can always add some frills later. Think of it like buying a basic car. A lot of the accessories are extras you can at least temporarily live without. However, you may be surprised to discover you actually enjoy simplicity and don't want to return to the land of consumption.

Action Steps – Questions to Ponder

What is the difference between a high standard of living and a high quality of life?

Quality of life has more to do with the surroundings we choose to live in, the time we have to spend with friends and family, access to nature, homegrown food, places to walk or hike, pets, and a strong sense of community. There are many places in the world that have a low standard of living but a high quality of life. Of course, it is possible to have both.

For every activity you participate in, ask yourself: will this improve the quality of my life?

How much money do you need each month to support your current lifestyle?

Are your possessions a burden or do they contribute to your happiness?

If you use and enjoy them, keep them. If not, release them so someone else can use them. Don't allow unused possessions to weigh you down. Clear out items you don't love or haven't used in the past year. This will give you space to breathe and create, while providing room for things you will love and use. Give away any surplus items to someone who can truly use them. Practice keeping your life simple and uncomplicated.

There are three main ways to increase your income. Which would you prefer?

Spend less, get a job that pays more, or add a second stream of income. There are many low-cost self-employment options to get you started quickly even while working full-time. See The $100 Startup *or Google other ideas (see below).*

Consider bartering, co-op buying clubs, co-op housing, working co-operatives, and simple sharing of resources such as tools you already own.

Determine the amount of money you will need to save before you can pursue work on your own terms. This will focus you to save more quickly.

Set a target date.

To maintain your motivation, set the date no longer than three years from now. (I ate a lot of peanut butter and jelly in the six months prior to spending a year backpacking through Europe.) When you are motivated, you will endure a little short-term pain for long-term gain.

Keep in mind, this is not a retirement plan. It is your "new way of working" plan. Once you can live within your means, you will be able to relax and allow greater financial freedom to emerge.

Soundtrack

While writing this chapter, the song "What a Wonderful World" by Louis Armstrong was playing in my mind.

Books You Might Like to Read

Your Money or Your Life
by Joe Dominguez and Vicki Robin

Money and the Meaning of Life
by Jacob Needleman

Voluntary Simplicity
by Duane Elgin

The $100 Startup
by Chris Guillebeau

Put Work in Its Place
by Bruce O'Hara

Also Google

Voluntary Simplicity

Chapter 5:
The Heart Of The Matter

How might work, freed from the drivers for power and success that have dominated men (and now women) through midlife, serve the evolving needs of human life in these new years of age?

Betty Friedan

Intrinsic life goals and the creation of meaning appear to be central to coping with our own mortality.

William S. Breitbart

Plato, quoting Socrates, said: "The unexamined life is not worth living." The only way to attain self-awareness is through self-reflection—something that our busy modern lifestyle often does not have time for.

If you feel life is pushing and pulling you in all directions and you can't keep up, clearly you don't know where you are going. The way to choose a direction is to focus on your core values and then choose to live them in both your life and work.

In examining our life choices, we need to confront our values. Identify your beliefs about what is most important in your life. What exactly is it that you value? Authenticity is when our public and private selves are the same. We have no need to wear a mask.

Robert Frost was speaking of personal choice when he wrote

"Two roads diverged in a wood, and I—
I took the one less traveled by,
And that has made all the difference."

What we valued in our youth is likely very different from our midlife values. I was first alerted to a contrast in values when I worked as a group leader of twelve youths. Even just a ten-year age difference created a huge gap in what we found important. The group norm was to place the highest value on sex, alcohol, drugs, and loud music above all else. It was a challenge playing the role of "den mother" to that group. At age thirty, I felt a huge chasm in our values.

If you are unclear what your values are, look at how you spend your money, time, and energy as they usually go toward what is important to you. We tend to associate with people who share our values. It's likely essential for any long-term relationship.

Whenever we experience conflict in a job, it may be our values are out of alignment with our work. A vegetarian is unlikely to be found working in a slaughter house. A less obvious contrast in values occurs when an independent spirit works for a micromanaging boss. Fireworks are sure to follow. We feel fulfilled when our core values are met. A common midlife need is to fully express our core values in our work.

It would be wonderful, if as with potted plants, we came with instructions on how to be cared for to ensure we would blossom. Since we don't, now is the time to self-nurture. Fulfilling your own needs is how you can also benefit others. Keep in mind that cravings are not needs. Cravings are like junk food that never provides long-term satisfaction but rather are a short-term fix for the nutrition we really need. Our true needs arise from our authentic self. If you were an actor auditioning for the role of your authentic self, what would that look like? Would you give a convincing performance?

Each of us gets to choose what our core values are. They differ from person to person. They are like stars on a cloudy night. Even if we can't see them, we know they are there. Our gut feelings can provide helpful guidance in choosing the things we value most. Once we understand what really matters to us, we need to act on it—with our eyes wide open.

A values-based life does not depend on others for approval. We are likely to face rejection along the way. A life of integrity means we are 100 percent committed to living our values. Without this, any roadblocks might appear insurmountable. Your values need to matter more than any roadblocks. Pain is often a part of living a life we truly care about.

What motivates your work?
I watched a speech given by career analyst and author Daniel Pink on TED TV. He said it is now clear that the carrot-and-stick approach that uses external motivators like monetary bonuses does not work. What does motivate people to unleash their productivity are intrinsic rewards, three in particular: *Autonomy*—we have a need to direct our own lives; *Mastery*—a desire to learn, create, or master new things; *Purpose*—a desire to better ourselves and our world.

This has been tested extensively all over the world over the past forty years, in both rich and poor countries, and the results have been the same. Financial incentives and rewards often led to a negative impact on performance of tasks that require creativity. The reasoning is that both rewards and punishments often remove the innate desire to do the work for its own sake. Surprisingly, much of the work world has yet to recognize this reality.

Bob Proctor says the purpose of all human organizations should be to make life more meaningful. He suggests we make lifestyle choices and contribution to others the main focus of our lives. He says that people are spiritual beings living in physical bodies and the only creatures on earth that are not totally at home in their own environment because they have the option of creating it for themselves, but often choose not to (Proctor, 1984).

Plants and animals live in the environment they are placed in. Have you consciously chosen the lifestyle you want to lead and the environment you want to live it in? When we don't have an internal compass to guide us, it is hard to find our "North Star." To create a life consistent with your values, you first need to identify them. When our activities don't mesh with our deepest values, we feel lost in meaningless busyness.

When personal values are out of sync with workplace values, stress levels rise. If your work does not match your values, it will likely feel meaningless, no matter how outwardly successful you might look. A mismatch will drain rather than energize you.

When you think of your future work, which will you value more:

External or Internal motivators?

External Motivators—rewards usually given to us by others

- high income
- health care coverage
- fringe benefits / job perks
- job security
- bonuses / raises
- getting an A+ on your job review
- corner office
- status / prestige
- awards
- pension plan
- gold watch
- possibility of promotion

Internal Motivators—come from within and often linked to our feelings

- integrity / authenticity — born out of self-knowledge
- sense of belonging / self-respect

- enjoying the process of using your potential
- working with flow / joy
- curiosity / opportunity to express creativity
- good health / emotional well-being / optimism
- intellectual challenge / lifelong learning
- self-actualization / meaningful work
- personal growth / spiritual growth
- freedom / autonomy / independence / flexibility
- mastery—able to overcome a personal challenge
- purpose / legacy / making a difference
- opportunity to make the world a better place
- service to others—a need to give back to society

External factors have a limited effect on our happiness. Yet, external rewards are what most of us have chased after. Keep in mind the truth in a statement from Helen Keller who said that "security is mostly a superstition." Defining ourselves by our external values will leave us feeling empty in the end.

Think about someone like Gandhi or Nelson Mandela. Mandela spent twenty-six years in jail because of his values. Despite his confinement, he felt he was free to live life on his own terms. Viktor Frankl described a similar choice in *Man's Search for Meaning*. He had an opportunity to escape the concentration camps, but instead, he chose to stay imprisoned with his patients. He experienced that moment as both free and peaceful because he had chosen to do what mattered to him. Most of us will not do anything quite as dramatic, but on some level we each face similar choices as to how we live our values.

Those who work because they are motivated by internal rewards are harder to control than those motivated by external rewards. The work becomes its own reward. What do you do when you are internally motivated? Does it differ when you are externally motivated?

The key to internal motivation is your interest in what you are learning. Success is the result of doing what interests you. If the process of doing your work fascinates you, the outcome becomes a bonus gift. If the end result depends on others or circumstances that are beyond your control, the likelihood of success decreases. Take the opportunity that helps you grow.

When you know what you are against—turn it around so you are clear about what you stand for. You may have heard the saying, "If you don't know what you stand for, you'll fall for anything." This is a good reminder. What do you stand for?

Recognize that security can only truly come from within. You cannot get it outside of yourself. Could it be our own insecurity that is creating insecurity in the world—not the other way around? To change the world, perhaps we need to change ourselves. If we nourish our own lives, we can better nourish others. Whenever we do something that raises our life energy, we raise the life energy of the world.

If you have trouble choosing your core values, try visualizing what is most important to you. Put your values in order of priority. Try combining your top values. Selling out to what is convenient is a poor compromise. Living in alignment with our values often requires effort and a willingness to face pain that is similar to a mother giving birth. The end result makes it all worthwhile. Don't allow fear to hold you back. Not living life on your own terms will hurt you more. As people like Nelson Mandela and Viktor Frankl have shown, even if imprisoned, if we live our values, we will always be free.

Which causes do you support?
Author Stephen King said of Baby Boomers: "We had a chance to change the world and opted for the Home Shopping Channel instead." The Dalai Lama said, "Spirituality, understood as a return to essential human values, is the key to our survival . . . inner transformation can lead to transforming the world."

I see Boomers longing to share what they've learned and reconnecting with their desire to change the world. Venture philanthropy is one of the top trends in British charity work. I am choosing to express my values in the causes I support. There are two I am particularly drawn to. One is international, KIVA, an organization that provides small-scale loans so women (and men) in Third World countries can start their own businesses. The other is in my home community, The Gabriola Commons, a grassroots organization that nourishes the social fabric of our community.

The future of work will favour those who are self-directed, intuitive, independent, and optimistic, who recognize our interdependence and our need to form mutually beneficial relationships. Midlife should reflect our values, beliefs, priorities, and insights in a meaningful way. Lasting happiness requires us to find our core strengths and figure out how to put them to work.

Action Steps – Questions to Ponder

What are your Core Values—that give meaning to your life? *They are always internal, not external.*

Are you living them? How has not living your values impacted your life?

Which values do you refuse to compromise?

What needs to change if you are not living your core values?

Do your family, friends, and workplace share your values?

Our future is based on making conscious choices and then taking personal responsibility for living them. Use your values like an internal GPS so you will be alerted if you stray off-course.

List your motivators for your work. They may come from both lists: *External and Internal Motivators.*

Will you have the strength of mind to handle any roadblocks that come between you and the life you want to lead?

What goals have you set for yourself?

Until you know where you want to go, you can't define the steps to get there. Without goals, there is no action, only daydreams.

Once you have set a goal, ask yourself:

Is this what I really want?

Is it consistent with my core values?

Am I able to take ownership and responsibility to achieve it?

Will I enjoy the process as much as the end result?

Have I set a target date to achieve it?

I like to have clients create a portable Soul Card (separate from a Vision Board) that depicts their Core Values with words and pictures. I suggest they consult it before making any major decisions. It is important to have our decisions align with our values if we are to live a life of integrity. Whenever we are at a crossroad in our lives, our values can point us in the right direction. They help prioritize how we spend our time. Live your life in conscious connection with your values.

What do you want your life to stand for?

What energizes and excites you about the future?

What will fulfill you most at this time in your life?

Create a *Personal Mission Statement* that provides focus and direction based on your core values:

This is my Mission Statement: I help Boomer women to live and work on their own terms in midlife and beyond.

Books You Might Like to Read

Dibs In Search of Self
by Virginia M. Axline

Drive
by Daniel Pink

Man's Search for Meaning
by Viktor Frankl

The Purpose Driven Life
by Rick Warren

The Authentic Career
by Maggie Craddock

Our Clinic: Visionary Health Care, Fundraising and Community Building on Gabriola Island
by Bruce Mason

Also Google

www.philanthropyuk.org

KIVA
www.kiva.org

Gabriola Commons
www.gabriolacommons.ca

Chapter 6:
Success Wears Many Colours

Success is measured not so much by the position that one has reached in life as by the obstacles which one has overcome while trying to succeed.

Booker T. Washington

We need to "know ourselves"
Clients often told me they "didn't know what they wanted to be when they grew up"—even when in their fifties. I felt that my job was to help them find out. The problem was that my larger mandate was to just get people off government assistance and into a job. It didn't matter if the job was a good fit. There was little time for introspection. Self-exploration is a process that is not often encouraged by family, school, society, or the media and so is largely ignored by many who simply fall into a job based on the desires of those around them or what is available at the time. I hope you are taking the time to look inside at what you really want.

What is your meaning of success?
What must your life be like for you to feel successful? The Oxford dictionary definition of success is "the attainment of fame, wealth, or social status." Do we really crave having paparazzi chasing after us to take pictures during our private moments? That's often the result of fame. If no photographer is present, sometimes we feel compelled to post our own photos on social media. What are we really craving?

Western culture tends to define success in terms of money, fame, and power, and this is also how advertisers sell a lot of products. Our unconscious choices sometimes get us suckered into buying things we don't really need due to this definition of success.

For ten years, Richard St. John was a researcher, marketing guru, and CEO speech writer. He has run over fifty marathons, climbed two of the world's highest mountains, has a black belt in judo, and has cycled halfway around the world. He became a millionaire doing what he loved.

Richard teaches what he believes creates a successful life. He says we need to have fun while working at what we love, to push ourselves to our limit so we can give others something of value, to be persistent, and to constantly improve ourselves. I'll add that we need to keep learning and collaborating with others. We need to evolve and manage future complexity by expanding our mindset. We are successful when we enjoy doing our best work that contributes to enhancing our planet.

I believe each of us needs to define success based on our intrinsic values. Dying with more possessions than everyone else seems unrewarding. Let's share what we have while alive.

Success is the peace of mind that comes from knowing we did our best. If we are in a job we don't enjoy, it likely means we are seeking external rewards. When we do the work we love, it becomes its own reward. I'm happiest when I am able to shine some light so others can find their way to their own "best" work.

Love, happiness, and success are all choices. These three tend to control and give power to the rest of our choices. To choose love, you first need to believe you are capable of both giving and finding it. To choose happiness, you have to believe it is part of your birthright. To choose success, you have to believe you deserve it.

If you define success from the perspective of your authentic self, it will lead you toward your best way to serve others. To be successful, make the decision to start believing in what is possible for you. Stop focusing on what you cannot do. It is not the rest of the world that holds us back. It is our disbelief in our own potential. From early infancy, most of us have been told what we cannot do. Many of us believe it. Release worry, stress, and fear. They do not serve you. Successful people believe in themselves. Only you can determine how successful you will be.

Maggie Craddock, author of *The Authentic Career*, believes "we tend to tap into the energy of the authentic self at the chronological age we reached when our true selves went into hibernation." Now's the time to wake up! Black Elk, medicine and holy man, said, "there is hope if people will begin to awaken that spiritual part of themselves—that heartfelt acknowledgement that we are the caretakers of life on this planet." Career Intuitive Sue Frederick says we need to "operate from a feeling of optimism and inspiration. It's the only way to attract success."

Happiness and success are born from our ability to work with purpose and meaning. My personal definition of success is having the freedom to use my creativity and passion in a way that makes a meaningful difference.

What reasons do you give for not being successful on your own terms?

I don't have the time.
I don't have enough education.
I'm just not lucky.
I can't afford it.
I have a family to support.
I'm too old.
I didn't inherit any money.
Other people wouldn't like it.
It's too risky.
Nobody will give me a break.
I'm too shy.
It's too hard.
I don't believe I deserve it. (*Probably the most accurate belief.*)

These are all just beliefs we carry with us. They've been programmed into us. Start debugging your own internal computer system. These may have been excuses in the past, but now they are simply choices. Now you can choose something different.

Action Steps – Questions to Ponder

Which of your family's ideas about success have you internalized?

Has the media defined success for you? How?

What does success mean for you? Define it in your own words. (*Before you go looking for "success," be clear about what it means to you and why you chose that definition.*)

Is this the same as your definition for how to live the "good life" yourself?
Once you are able to harness the power of your subconscious mind and to live and work with love in a way that also benefits others, you will have found your success.

Write a letter to the future—to those who will come after you. Tell them what made your life a success.

What is it you love to do that can form the core of your work? Here's an easy test to see if you have already found your *"true livelihood"*: You love your work so much you would be willing to do it for free.

A man is a success if he gets up in the morning and goes to bed at night and in between does what he wants to do.

Bob Dylan

Chapter 7:
So Many Choices

Entering a profession because it looks promising or secure is the ultimate crapshoot . . . Even more damaging to our vocational development is the belief that work is nothing more than a way to earn money. Why should we commit a third—or more—of our time to doing something that we don't care about? Why can't we get paid for being happy?

Barbara J. Winter

Ken Dychwald, gerontologist and author, helped create The New Retirement Survey for financial management company, Merrill Lynch. It revealed that Baby Boomers will redefine the word "retirement" as most plan to retire from their current form of work at about age sixty-four, only to start a different form of work with an intention to alternate between work and leisure. Two-thirds want to work for the mental stimulation and challenge; the others because they will need the money. Boomers who already have a plan and feel prepared are twice as optimistic as those without one (Dychwald, 2013).

The times I've felt the most trapped in my life were the times when I was unable to see any options. While we always have options, we don't always realize we have them. The reason I promote Voluntary Simplicity is because it will give you the freedom to explore your options.

Barbara J. Winter, a popular public speaker across Canada and the United States, has been encouraging audiences to develop multiple sources of income for the past few decades. She feels that by creating our own work we can live more balanced lives.

In her inspiring book, *Making a Living Without a Job*, Winter suggests we develop what she calls "multiple profit centres." She advises creating more than one source of income—some funds perhaps from a part-time job, some from a pension, and some income from self-employment, based on a hobby we love. Performing volunteer work is another avenue in which to connect with others and give back. Having multiple sources of income provides a better sense of security than relying on the traditional one-job, one-paycheque we have been accustomed to.

We need to start thinking of ourselves as self-employed, even if we currently have a job in someone else's company. This is how we remain employable. We invest in our own research and development by observing the trends for our chosen industry and continually upgrade our skills. We only fully commit to this when we truly love our work. Remaining in a job you don't enjoy seems riskier to me than making a well-planned move toward something you love. Consider how you can serve someone else's unmet needs. If you choose to become an entrepreneur, it may take a while for the money to follow, but at least you will enjoy the process.

Once the mortgage is paid off and the kids have left home, Boomers are free to start weighing their options. If you have a company pension—great—but many don't. If you are old enough to receive it, a government pension can provide a base income. You might want to seek advice on what age would be best for you to start receiving a pension.

You owe it to yourself to have more than one source of income. If you enjoy your current line of work, see if you can reduce your hours by working either part-time or on a freelance basis. If you need a change of career, you might want to find a part-time job to provide a base income before you explore other options.

The service industry provides the greatest number of job opportunities, although many positions pay only minimum wage.

Seasonal tourism jobs are an attractive option for many mature workers who enjoy summer or winter activities. If you work at a golf club or ski resort, you will have access to those sports in your downtime, and it will likely be cost-free.

Once you have income from a pension and/or a part-time job, you will then have a chance to explore some form of self-employment. If you had three sources of income, you would likely feel more secure about your future, alleviating most of the perceived "fear factor." I think the most fun and rewarding work, both emotionally and financially, comes from self-employment. I highly recommend this route. It will become your best avenue for self-development. It also allows you to connect with a wide variety of fascinating people.

Born to be a free agent
When Daniel Pink began talking about the "free agent nation," a lot of people were paying attention. A 2004 University of Zurich survey of workers in twenty-three countries revealed the self-employed to be substantially more satisfied than those who worked for someone else, even when they were working longer hours and earning less money. Many report they are now grateful to have been laid off as it gave them a chance to try something new.

Our jobs often determine what our lives are like. With fewer responsibilities in midlife, we get to choose our lifestyle preference first and then fit our work around it. More and more Boomers are choosing to be re-birthed as free agents.

What is a free agent?
Free agents work as consultants, freelancers, temps, or as solopreneurs or micropreneurs. Their numbers are on the rise. Some choose this route due to dysfunctional workplaces, layoffs, or lifestyle choices. Do you admire the Hollywood lifestyle? It epitomizes free-agent status. Writers, actors, directors, and all other film crew members work exclusively on short-term contracts.

Although it seems counterintuitive, free-agent status offers more security than working in a regular job. Corporate lifespans are shrinking. With a regular job, you can be let go at any time. Having a variety of projects, clients, customers, or employers to work for is likely to spread out your income-generating ability and hedge your bets if one of them no longer requires your services.

Being your own boss will enable you to pursue projects that can satisfy a deeper yearning to make a difference, rather than just a living. It will allow you to live authentically both on and off the job. You can be the same person at work that you are at home. No more need to muzzle yourself during staff meetings. You will succeed or fail on your own merit. Administrators won't squash your ideas. No more office politics.

You can define success on your own terms. You can choose who to work with. Hire other free agents to perform the tasks you'd rather not do yourself. Socialize with other solopreneurs to share ideas and enjoy each other's company. Want every Friday off? Do it. Want two months vacation every year? Plan your work around that.

Free-agent status will enable you to create a new system in which to work that supports your own image. Whether you choose free-agent status on a full-time or part-time basis, I believe it's your best option. Project-based or temporary work is becoming more common among older workers, fitting in with a desire for more flexible part-time work schedules. Becoming a free agent will help you to regain control and power over your own life.

If you do not see yourself as an entrepreneur, you may want to join forces with someone who is. Sole proprietors never make it alone. They always seek out others to provide the skills they lack. If you are familiar with the personality assessment tool called the Myers-Briggs Type Indicator, you will recognize the premise that we need all types to run the world. Whatever we are strong at has its opposite weakness. It is those weaknesses we hire others for. Although there is merit in developing your weaknesses, it makes a lot more sense to spend most of your time using your strengths.

There are a number of factors enabling people to work on their own terms today. Technology and global connection to the Internet has probably had the biggest impact on portable employment options. Outsourcing of work has meant both layoffs as well as more work being contracted out to individuals and small business. The number of solopreneurs has grown considerably and is popularized on TV shows such as *Shark Tank* and *Dragon's Den*. Niche consumer markets and customized products are more in demand.

Both Canadian and American studies reveal that about 25 percent of new entrepreneurs are aged fifty-five to sixty-four, with some in their eighties. Numerous studies in both countries indicate that more than half of all Boomers expect to work in retirement and their preferred choice is self-employment (Culp, 2009; Hipple, 2010). There is a huge increase in freelancers doing business with other freelancers. The website, Elance, is one on-line example of how Boomers are connecting with each other and working together via the Internet.

You may prefer to work alongside others. The United Nations declared 2012 the International Year of Co-operatives. More people are becoming aware of this alternate work model. Co-ops extend democracy by shifting decision-making power from a top-down management style to decisions made by community members. Many co-ops are owned by their consumers, such as the outdoor sports gear company, Mountain Equipment Co-op (now called MEC). Others are owned and operated by the people who work for them. Farmer and artist co-ops are ones we are most familiar with.

In my region, several diverse new co-ops have recently been formed, including a TV station, pulp and paper mill, and furniture store that are all either wholly or partially employee-owned and operated. Would a worker co-op work for you?

Statistics Canada noted the 2008-2009 increase in self-employed workers was mainly due to people aged fifty-five plus, with women accounting for 58 percent of the increase overall. A report from the Ewing Marion Kauffman Foundation revealed Americans aged fifty-five to sixty-four had a higher rate of entrepreneurial activity than workers between the ages of twenty to thirty-four, every year from 1996 to 2007. This trend shows no sign of slowing down (Ewing Marion Foundation, 2012; LaRochelle-Cote, 2010).

Older entrepreneurs seem to be more clear about who they are, what they like to do, and why they want to do it along with who they want to serve.

Start to think like an entrepreneur
Whether you are considering self-employment or not, start to think like an entrepreneur. The first step might be unlearning how to be a good employee. Once you are self-employed, you can have as much variety and as many profit centres as you like. You will not just care about your work, but will know why you are doing it and believe it has value that goes further than having a steady paycheque. It will provide you with the ultimate self-growth program.

Employees commiserate; entrepreneurs brainstorm.

Alice Barry

I believe the world would be a better place if we were all self-employed—or at least acted as if we were. It would encourage us to continually assess our skills and keep them current. This would enhance our self-esteem, problem-solving ability, creativity, passion, purpose and meaning. It would push us to maximize our talents and develop any neglected interests and abilities. We know the world needs more creative solutions to emerging problems. Above all, working at something you love and enjoying your life is a gift to the world. Pass it on.

Action Steps – Questions to Ponder

Do you have a preference for how you want to work in the future?

Have you explored all of your options?

Books You Might Like to Read

Making a Living Without a Job
by Barbara J. Winter

Creating You & Company
by William Bridges

Free Agent Nation
by Daniel Pink

Also Google

Ashoka

Ashoka connects social entrepreneurs. It suggests that everyone can be a "changemaker" and that people have the power of transformation. All social change begins with the belief that change is possible. The strategy it uses is combining the business world with the social world—Ashoka states this is the future of business. Businesses that don't address the social world will lose out. Citizens will demand it. Generation Y has already joined this movement.

Some of the world banks recognize this and are getting involved with the micro-financing of small businesses. The leader in this field is the Grameen Bank. Social entrepreneurs are determined they'll get through closed doors and create change by using their skills to do what's right for others.

Other options to explore:

- job sharing
- contract worker
- consultant
- worker co-ops
- virtual partnerships

New words to describe different ways to work are popping up every day. Keep in mind the lifestyle you would like to lead as you explore your options.

II.
FEAR OF CRITICISM

Chapter 8:
Think For Yourself

Your time is limited, so don't waste it living someone else's life . . . Don't let the noise of other's opinions drown out your own inner voice. And, most important, have the courage to follow your heart and intuition.

Steve Jobs

The more authentically and creatively you live your life, the more people will suggest that you calm down or not rock the boat. But telling the human spirit to calm down is like asking water to run upstream.

Denise Bissonnette

Don't live for the approval of others. You'll never please everyone, regardless of what you do. As you read through the following chapters, imagine living life from a different perspective and take away anything that might be useful to your own life.

Barbara Winter taught me to "work with the willing." Ignore the critics. Recognize when what others say has merit, but reject criticism from detractors who are prompted by a lack of courage to live life on their own terms. I have been criticized for trying to change things for a way I believe will better serve others. I'm willing to take those hits because I truly believe my own path is better for me and will ultimately also help many midlife career changers.

I have also been criticized for my ability to "hunker down" and focus on the task at hand. Sustained focus is the best way to accomplish anything. Focus helps you attain your goals. If your mind is hopping all over the place, will you get anything done? This is why multi-tasking has now been proven inefficient.

Is it essential for you to keep up with the latest fashions? Are you concerned people will snicker behind your back if you wear last year's colours or don't drive the latest model car? Advertisers hope so. They want you to fear other's opinions so you will buy, buy, buy whatever they are selling whether you need it or not.

Perhaps our fear of criticism stems from hearing about martyrs who have been burned at the stake for their beliefs. Hopefully, by the time you reach midlife, you have not only formed your own opinions but will readily express them.

If you've experienced criticism from family, teachers, or employers—now is the time to have your own voice heard. Criticism can plant fear, compliance, and resentment in people. It is almost as feared as poverty. Feed your mind positive thoughts. You've likely heard the saying, "Garbage in, garbage out."

I have a bit of a perverse belief about criticism. I tend to accept it as proof that I am growing and thinking for myself. Criticism tends to help me think more deeply about my ideas. Sometimes it will help me change my mind. At other times it strengthens my beliefs. Sometimes, I'll assume an opposing view and play with it, just to try it on for size to see if it is a better fit for me. I suggest you try this. It's really the purpose of this book. Have fun with this idea.

At the same time, we need to protect our mind as if it were a million-dollar gold mine—because it is. David J. Schwartz, author of *The Magic of Getting What You Want*, reminds us that all we are and all we have in this life—our sense of self, of joy and sharing, our aspirations, our connectedness to the world—have their origins in our minds.

The media is a dominant influence over what we think and how we behave. All advertisers know this. TV is now one long series of commercials with a bit of filler shows in between. (*Guess that is why it is called commercial TV as opposed to Public Service television.*) What kind of media do you feed your brain? There are numerous positive things happening in the world, yet the media focus is primarily on the negative—the more disastrous, sensational, or gory it seems, the more coverage it gets.

How hollow are our lives that we devour Hollywood gossip as if it's free candy we can't get enough of? What kind of hunger are we feeding when we find it necessary to view photos of a topless future Queen? What value do we get in exchange for the cost of the magazines that carry these images?

What does it say about the state of our minds when popular culture creates hit shows like *Jersey Shore, Big Brother, and Toddlers and Tiaras?* The list goes on. Are these good role models for us?

When the media feeds us a steady diet of "bad economy" stories, small businesses suffer. Don't buy into it. These stories not only drive the economy down further, but they're not true. I believe the quote from Ralph Waldo Emerson, "This time, like all times, is a very good one, if we but know what to do with it."

Your mind is your best asset; protect it from negative influences. What are your own moods and emotions telling you? Feelings of boredom, irritability, frustration, anger or sadness are all red flags indicating a need to pay attention to the root cause. If you are the one who is criticizing the world around you, it is even more essential to make a change. Life is meant to be enjoyed. You need to figure out how to create a joy-filled life for yourself. I don't believe anyone wants to lie on their deathbed thinking, "Thank God that's over!"

As you read through the following chapters, imagine living life from each different perspective offered. We tend to get stuck in our own mindsets. This is a chance to look at the world through different eyes. Make a note of any ideas that might be useful in your own life.

Action Steps – Questions to Ponder

Who is calling the shots in your life?

Whose criticism do you most fear?

Book you might like to read:

The Magic of Getting What You Want
by David J. Schwartz

Chapter 9:
Live Like A Europeon

If you are lucky enough to have lived in Paris as a young man, then wherever you go for the rest of your life, it stays with you, for Paris is a moveable feast.

Ernest Hemingway

If you have never been to Europe (*or, like me, it has unfortunately been decades since you were there*), let's have a look at what we might learn from their way of life.

Lots of leisure time

What is most surprising for most North Americans is the amount of leisure time Europeans have. A typical vacation (*every year— not just a special one*) is six, eight, or twelve weeks off work. Each year, North Americans spend about two months more time at work than the Germans. Do we really believe poet David Whyte when he says, "Work is not and never has been the centre of the human universe"?

Life in the slow lane

Europeans move at a slower pace (*with the exception of the Autobahn*). They are much more relaxed. I found that irritating when I first arrived in Spain, Italy, and Greece—especially when waiting in line to buy a train ticket while the clerk leisurely ate his lunch in front of me. Europeans will spend hours in the middle of a workday just sipping coffee at an outdoor café and people-watching. When I was in Spain, I was surprised I couldn't find anywhere open to get a meal between 2 and 7 p.m. They were all closed for siesta.

Arrive on a Sunday and nearly everything is locked up. They're off at the beach or enjoying some leisurely family time—definitely not off shopping at the mall. They enjoy life and place a lot of emphasis on the arts, relaxation, and spending time with family. At other times, I'd arrive at a museum late in the day, but before closing time, and be told to come back *mañana* (tomorrow) as there was not enough time to look around. It seemed as if everywhere I went, I would hear *mañana, mañana.* If you can't do it today, I'd be told, so what—you come back tomorrow. When I returned home, I had a T-shirt printed up with the word *mañana* emblazoned across the front. By then, I too was thinking, "Really, what's the big hurry? Slow down and savour each experience."

Small-scale living
Europeans live life on a much smaller scale. Most of the houses are small and close together (*what we might call quaint*). They have a lot less stuff in them, and no basements for the overflow. While visiting an English friend, I was embarrassed when she asked me to fetch the milk from the kitchen and I couldn't find the fridge. It was neatly tucked under a counter and looked like one of the cupboards—nothing like the monster fridges of home that come complete with ice machines.

They shop for most groceries (*with a wicker basket*) on a daily basis. And most of the produce is fresh. They walk and bike more. They use more public transit and enjoy hopping on either a bus or train. They drive smaller, more economical cars. Smart cars are all over Europe. They fit quite nicely on those small, winding cobblestone streets.

Forget the diet craze
Europeans eat well, but they eat less than most North Americans. They use full-fat milk in their coffee, eat butter-laden croissants and pour olive oil over both salads and pasta, but the portions are small— and besides—they walk a lot. They don't skip lunch or eat while working at their desk. They take a long lunch and enjoy it. It's hard to grab a bite to go as they don't use a lot of disposable plates or cutlery. They actually prefer to slow down and enjoy their food and drink while they socialize with family or friends.

Europeans tend to value the art of living, while North Americans appear more focused on work. Do North Americans really value money and stuff more than time? Is it the opposite for Europeans?

Action Steps – Questions to Ponder

How much stuff do you really need?
Last week I noticed a new building going up in town. It was yet another Storage Locker, available for monthly rental to house the stuff that won't fit in your basement or garage. Do we really need this much stuff?

Which do you prefer? Time or Money?

Are there any elements from the European way of life that you would like to incorporate into your own life? List them here.

Books You Might Like to Read

A Moveable Feast
by Ernest Hemingway

A Year in Provence
by Peter Mayle

Under the Tuscan Sun
by Frances Mayes

Also Google

Living and working in Europe

Chapter 10:
Geography Is Destiny

Where and how we live go a long way in determining who we are and who we become.

Winifred Gallagher

Imagine the difference between being born in New York City or being born in the Sahara Desert. How different would your life be if you had been born in China or beside the Amazon River?

I've made several major household moves in my life. I grew up in a small town, then moved to a big city for college and university. Twenty years ago, I relocated from Ontario to a small city on the West Coast of Canada, and more recently moved to a small Gulf island. Each location offered radically different opportunities for work and leisure.

Whenever I have asked newcomers to the West Coast why they chose to move here, the answer is invariably for the lifestyle. They like the slower pace of life, the climate, and the proximity to both the ocean and the forest. The fact that they also need to work is often an afterthought.

Elizabeth Gilbert's book, *Eat, Pray, Love*, provides a good example of how changing one's geography can alter one's destiny. For many years, where we worked determined both where and how we lived. Midlife is an opportunity to reverse that trend. The Information Age now enables many of us to live and work from any location with an Internet connection.

Where would you like to live, even for three months, to explore what life might offer you in a different location?
Even if you can't physically travel there right now, you can visit numerous Internet websites or borrow books and DVDs from your local library. What opportunities would be there for you? Who would you meet, which foods would you eat, and what would you do while there? Would a change of geography create other work options for you?

Travel remains a Boomer priority. Consider staying longer in one country, rather than a whirlwind trip to a number of different countries. It's much cheaper to rent by the month than it is by the day. Once you have been in a place for a few days, you'll be able to observe where the locals eat and shop. It's unlikely to be in high-priced tourist traps. To avoid costly roaming charges, you can buy a local pay-as-you-go mobile phone plan if you think you will need to make local calls. You can even arrange to trade your home with someone abroad. People have also traded RVs, rented one abroad or bought and then sold one at the end of their journey.

When you experience a different culture, you start to perceive life in a new way. If you have visited a country radically different from your own, you may have experienced the effect of culture shock once you returned home. I know I did. North America seemed too fast-paced and very wasteful after a year abroad. It can make you wonder if your own culture and society have shaped your perception in a way that might not fit your own true nature.

If you want to experience living full-time in a foreign country, there are still many places around the world you could move to and live on less than at home. If you were to relocate, you could do paid or volunteer work from a new location. You could get the credentials needed to teach English abroad. If you are physically fit, you might want to sign on as a WOOFER. In exchange for work on a farm, you will be given free room and board, as well as a local guide in the form of your host.

Do some research about countries you might like to explore in depth. In Panama City, you can live comfortably on less than $2,000 a month. In Chiang Mai, Thailand, $500 a month will rent you a furnished luxury condo. Ecuador and Mexico are also popular with both Canadians and Americans. Carefully weigh the pros and cons before moving to a foreign country and always check with your embassy to ensure the country has political stability. It's a good idea to test out the new location on a long-term basis prior to buying. Consider renting your current home out and then temporarily (or permanently) renting in your new location.

While many Boomers want to travel extensively across Canada and the United States, they still need to earn a living. Some have already figured out how to combine the two. There are full-time RVers who have sold their home, downsized considerably, and now work while on the road. I think of this as the updated Boomer version of hitchhiking through Europe. Only now, we take the kitchen sink on the road with us. However, living in an RV means you have more room in your life for experiences than you do for material goods.

I think Boomers are buying RVs to recapture the wanderlust they had in youth, satisfying their need for adventure, independence, and spontaneity. The lifestyle offers a chance to reconnect with the same group of people you backpacked through Europe with.

Keep in mind that it is the journey, not the destination that counts. So, enjoy the journey.

Soundtrack — from the movie Easy Rider

"Born to be Wild"
Steppenwolf (1969)

Get your motor runnin'
Head out on the highway
Lookin' for adventure
In whatever comes our way

Action Steps – Questions to Ponder

Has your work determined your lifestyle?

What lifestyle would you choose if you no longer had to work?

Where do you most want to live?
This might change over time.

Start with this list and add your own requirements to it.

Country / language spoken by the locals:

Climate:

City or Rural:

Type of community desired:

Easy access to outdoor recreation and the arts:

Close to an ocean, lake, river, mountain, desert, forest:

Portable home or permanent home?

Different location for each season?

Add your own requirements:

Real estate agents know it is all about "location, location, location."
Our geographic location really does strongly influence how we live.

Geography also refers to the environment we work in.
Why would you choose to continue to work in an environment that stifles your spirit?

Books You Might Like to Read

The Whole Earth Catalog
by Stewart Brand
(A 60s classic)

Lonely Planet Travel Guides
(Select by country)

Also Google

Rick Steves
Volunteer Vacations
Teach English Abroad
WWOOFER

Here's a good website for work opportunities while traveling:

www.travelocity.com/travelforgood

Chapter 11:
Teach Your Parents Well

If you see in any given situation only what everybody else can see, you can be said to be so much a representative of your culture that you are a victim of it.

S. I. Hayakawa

Is there anything Baby Boomers can learn from Generation Y? These are the children we gave birth to after 1979 and nurtured to believe they could be whatever they wanted to be.

They grew up with the constancy of advancing technology and the realization that nothing is static. They have always known they would need to manage their own careers. They don't expect to stay in any one job long-term, so as soon as they feel they have exhausted their learning with one organization, they move on to another. We taught the kids to "follow their dreams." Now they believe it is their birthright. Neither generation may trust the world economy, but maybe we can trust ourselves to rely on each other.

Dan Tapscott, author of *Grown up Digital*, says some of the common characteristics of Gen Y include being technologically savvy, comfortable with ethnic diversity, tenacious, optimistic, confident, goal-oriented, sociable, possessing strong morals and a sense of civic duty.

Do you want what Gen Y wants?

Gen Y wants
- workplace flexibility
- feedback on their work performance
- entrepreneurial opportunities
- meaningful work
- work/life balance
- freedom in everything they do
- the ability to personalize and customize products and services
- companies that operate with integrity, transparency, and openness
- ability to incorporate play into their work
- relationships and collaboration
- innovative companies where they can contribute ideas for improvement

Gen Y does not believe life is all about work. They want to be happy, give back to others, and enjoy life. This generation watched their parents work long hours and return home stressed. They have no desire to repeat this pattern. They network like crazy via social media because they feel relationship building is crucial and believe technology enables them to complete a job in half the time it might take an older worker who doesn't use it. They don't believe in hierarchy and will email anyone at any level if they want a question answered. They want and expect employers to hear what they have to say. They want to learn new skills and grow with their jobs. Personal satisfaction is often more important than overtime pay. This generation wants an open work environment that encourages initiative and allows them to have fun at work.

This group wants to be able to live up to their full potential and looks for workplaces to provide team building, variety, interesting jobs, and moral satisfaction. Some companies are bending over backwards to court this generation by taking their needs into account. The Telus Corporation is one of them. It provides workshops on Leadership Development as a way to move this group of employees up the corporate ladder.

Partnerships with youth seem like a perfect business marriage. Boomers have years of knowledge and experience; Gen Y has the know-how with current technology. We both want to improve world conditions. Once you have found your passion, you might want to look for youth who share it so you can combine your skills.

Boomers crave having the flexibility to be able to alternate between work and leisure. Many Boomers would love to job-share. Some like the idea of six months on and six months off. Pair them with someone who enjoys the opposite six months and you have a full-time position filled by two happy employees. Most employers are not yet onboard with this idea—but I'm sure they soon will be as this also appeals to Gen Y.

Action Steps – Questions to ponder

Is there anything you can learn from Generation Y?

Do you possess or wish to cultivate any of the common traits they possess?
Suggestion: Find a volunteer organization with younger people so you can enjoy their energy and expertise.

Soundtracks ♫

This is a song most Boomers will be familiar with.

"Teach Your Children Well"
Crosby, Stills, Nash & Young

Teach your parents well,
Their children's hell will slowly go by,
And feed them on your dreams,
The one they picks, the one you'll know by.

The following song, recommended by a friend, will be new to most Boomers as it is a Gen Y creation.

"When It Comes My Turn"
 David Myles

These words came to David when he experienced what he termed his "quarter-life crisis" at age twenty-five. He said Boomers often relate to it.

I'm getting old but I'm not old yet
I'm already worried that I might forget
How to laugh, how to love
How to live, how to learn
I want to die with a smile
When it comes my turn.

Book you might like to read:

Grown up Digital
by Dan Tapscott

Also Google

Generation Y at work

Chapter 12:
Olympic Athletes Believe They Can Fly

You miss 100 percent of the shots you don't take.

Wayne Gretzky, hockey player

For an athlete to make it to the podium at the Olympics, it takes many years of hard work. Many have shown incredible inner strength and determination to overcome injuries, illness, and psychological challenges. Elite athletes share a mindset, level of dedication, and perseverance that we could all learn from. They are passionate about their sport, intensely focused, and guided by their own instincts.

Our greatest journey is to discover and fulfill our human potential. This takes courage and persistence.

Silken Laumann, Silver and two Bronze, Rowing

He who is not courageous enough to take risks will accomplish nothing in life.

Muhammad Ali, Gold, Boxing

Each of us has a fire in our hearts for something. It's our goal in life to find it and keep it lit.

Mary Lou Retton, Gold, two Silver and two Bronze, Gymnastics

Never underestimate the power of dreams and the influence of the human spirit.

Wilma Rudolph, three Gold and one Bronze, Track and Field

If you dream and you allow yourself to dream, you can do anything.

Clara Hughes, Multiple Olympic medals, Cyclist and Speed Skater

Nothing is impossible. With so many people saying it couldn't be done, all it takes is an imagination.

Michael Phelps, eighteen Gold, Swimming

It's better to have a rich soul than to be rich.

Olga Korbut, four Gold and two Silver, Gymnastics

It is better to look ahead and prepare than to look back and regret.

Jackie Joyner-Kersee, three Gold, one Silver and two Bronze, Heptathalon

A lot of times when you go through a very traumatic situation and it's emotionally difficult to deal with, you come back spiritually stronger.

Elvis Stojko, two Silver, Figure Skating

Olympic Athletes Believe They Can Fly

Nobody needs to prove to anybody what they're worthy of—just the person they look at in the mirror.

Picabo Street, Gold and Silver, Downhill Skiing

Never put an age limit on your dreams.

Dara Torres, three Gold and two Silver, one Bronze, Swimming

I've failed over and over and over again in my life. And that is why I succeed.

Michael Jordon, two Gold, Basketball

When anyone tells me I can't do anything, I'm just not listening any more.

Florence Griffin Joyner, three Gold and two Silver, Track and Field

Money was never the motivation.

Katarina Witt, two Gold, Figure Skating

Believe in yourself. Have fun. Have an open mind. If you're not enjoying it, don't do it. Life's too short.

Debbie Meyer, three Gold, Swimming

I was passionate. I found something I loved.

Dorothy Hamill, Gold, Figure Skating

Olympic Athletes Believe They Can Fly

You have to believe in yourself when no one else does—that makes you a winner right there.

Venus Williams, three Gold, Tennis

You have to train your mind like you train your body.

Bruce Jenner, Gold, Decathalon

Olympic athletes get to the top of their game because they take advantage of things the rest of us could use. They have a coach. They visualize their end goal. They increasingly work to better themselves. They stay the course and practice their skills. They are persistent and dedicated to their own success. It was Wayne Gretzky who said, "Procrastination is one of the most common and deadliest of diseases, and its toll on success and happiness is heavy."

People who fail—think losing. People who win—think winning. Not everyone can win gold—but we can all achieve our personal best. Take educated risks. If you buy a new sailboat and insist on staying close to the shore, you'll never feel the power of the wind in your sails.

Develop persistent patience. Plant a seed and let it grow. Not everything in our world can be instant. Develop the patience to perfect what you do. I've heard it takes ten thousand hours of practice for a musician to become professional. (*I have fewer than fifty hours practicing the ukulele.*)

The easiest way to formulate a plan is to visualize what you want to achieve. As clearly as possible, picture in your mind's eye exactly what you would like to see happen in your life. Keep that image firmly in place until it manifests itself in reality. Maintain the faith that it will come true.

Olympic Athletes Believe They Can Fly

Action Steps – Questions to Ponder

What vision do you have of your future?

Review the quotes of the Olympians.
Find one that inspires you. Write it down and carry it with you to re-read whenever you need to refocus.

Draft your own *Motto to Live By.*
Carry that with you and read it regularly.

Who can you ask to be your Cheerleader or Mentor?
If the answer is not immediate, keep looking.

Books You Might Like to Read

Many athletes write books of their life stories and the odds they have overcome along the road to success. Choose a sport you enjoy and research who has written on that topic. Examples of athletes who have made heroic comebacks include Bethany Hamilton (surfer), Monica Seles (tennis player), and Scott Hamilton (figure skater).

Chapter 13:
Eccentrics Have More Fun

He who joyfully marches rank and file has already earned my contempt. He has been given a large brain by mistake, since for him the spinal cord would suffice.

Albert Einstein

That so few now dare to be eccentric, marks the chief danger of our time.

John Stuart Mill

The English are not just known for bad food. (*Having grown up with my mother's cooking, I can attest to that.*) They also have a reputation for a fondness for eccentricity. It is something that has always intrigued me about my heritage, so I was delighted to discover a society called The Eccentric Club, with its patron being HRH Prince Philip, Duke of Edinburgh.

Although the focus of the club is on social events and charity work, the Eccentric Club's website states: "We believe that it is essentially important to highlight and celebrate the eccentricity itself, as it was understood by our predecessors—an innate ability to ignore the well-trodden routes of the others and invent our own original ways." The club promotes creative and original approaches which may be considered controversial by present-day media and society.

For centuries, the club served as a meeting ground for many great and original minds, pioneers of thought in artistic, literary, theatrical, scientific, legal, and political circles. It provided a testing ground for novel and controversial theories and approaches important for all mankind. Some well-known eccentrics include Albert Einstein, Howard Hughes, Alexander Graham Bell, and Emily Dickinson.

Psychologist David Weeks, author of *Eccentrics*, has conducted research on eccentrics. He discovered they possess a number of similar traits, which include being non-conforming, creative, curious, idealistic, and opinionated. They also possess a mischievous sense of humour and are happily obsessed with one or more hobbies.

He learned too that they are both happier and healthier than most other people—likely because they are unconcerned with whether society approves or disapproves of their habits or beliefs. Weeks asserts that we can learn from eccentrics to "hold onto the dreams and curiosity we had as children." Above all, eccentrics choose to live life on their own terms, which is something we can all strive for. Consider the words of Niels Bohr: "If an idea does not appear bizarre, there is no hope for it."

Eccentrics can also teach us how to nurture our own eccentricity. Greater wisdom and inner strength always go to those who are willing to take a risk. John C. Maxwell, Christian author of *How Successful People Think*, noted "people often forget that you can't improve and still stay the same. Growth means change. Culture has taught us to value conformity over authenticity. Change requires challenging the status quo." Be willing to go against the grain. Innovation can be disruptive. Safety does not create new solutions.

Take a conscious risk that involves choosing to do what rings true for you, regardless of the initial discomfort it may cause. Always reach just beyond what you believe you are capable of. On the other side of conscious risk is the realization that who you really are has nothing to fear. To discover this, you first must face your fear. (*This is part of our Hero's Journey explored in the next chapter.*)

It was Robert F. Kennedy who popularized George Bernard Shaw's statement: "Some people see things as they are and say, 'Why?' I dream of things that never were and say, 'Why not?'" Challenge the status quo.

It is not just eccentrics who are unique. We all are. It's just that eccentrics are less inhibited about expressing their uniqueness. Someone once said to me, "If you don't think someone else is weird, it's because you don't know them very well." How well do you know your own weird self? What makes you unique? We all have a story to tell.

Do not fear to be eccentric in opinion for every opinion now accepted was once eccentric.

Bertrand Russell

Action Steps – Questions to Ponder

Do you possess any of the traits of eccentrics?

Which of these traits would you choose to nurture?

Could you accept the disapproval of others?

What annoys you? Can you work at improving the situation?

Would you be happier if you lived your life without concern about what others think?

See if you can find an eccentric in your neighbourhood. Arrange to chat with him or her.

Books You Might Like to Read

Eccentrics
by David Weeks

A Brit Different:
A guide to the eccentric events and curious contests of Britain
by Emma Woods

Also Google

The Eccentric Club
www.eccentricclub.co.uk
"Celebrating Eccentricity since 1781"

Re-watch the 1975 cult classic movie:

The Stepford Wives
Do not imitate them.

Chapter 14:
Your Hero's Journey

What's your "yes"? What you stand for is more important than what you are against. What's your path with heart?

Carlos Castenada

I was watching the film version of Joseph Campbell's *The Hero's Journey* when it occurred to me that this is the journey we are all on. We just choose different paths. Like any good story, we all have a beginning, a middle and an end. We're all here to slay our dragons before we leave this mortal plane and we each have the opportunity to be "reborn" in our present lifetime.

Campbell was an American mythologist, writer, and lecturer who coined the phrase, "follow your bliss." He taught that this is primarily a journey to the centre of yourself, an inner journey to wholeness and understanding, and that it's possible to view your entire life as a hero's journey. Campbell defined a hero as "an individual who does the best of things in the worst of times." A hero has the courage to listen to her own internal wisdom.

As Campbell explains, the journey begins with a Call to Adventure. This is the time when we notice that everything is about to change—whether we go willingly or not. We may refuse this call out of a sense of duty, fear, insecurity, or any number of other reasons. (*Have you ever known it was time to leave a job but felt that something was holding you back?*)

Once committed to the quest, a guide appears to help us cross the First Threshold, leaving the known limits of our world and venturing into the unknown. (*This book is meant to be your guide.*) The next step is into the Belly of the Whale—away from the known world and self and into the new world and new self. It is symbolized by something dark, unknown, and frightening. By entering this stage, we show a willingness to undergo a transformation, allowing our old self to fade away.

We are then led down a Road of Trials where we often stumble and fail a number of times. Along the way we encounter a number of temptations that try to lead us astray. (*This could be a high-paid job opening in a field you don't enjoy.*) Eventually, we are confronted with whatever holds the ultimate power in our life which prevents us from fulfilling our quest. For our transformation to be complete, we must slay this dragon (fear) that is blocking our way. Once successful, we will find our bliss.

For me, the Holy Grail we are seeking is our Purpose in Life, and the dragons we slay are our fears. Our journey ends with an integration of wisdom by achieving a balance between the material and spiritual worlds. This leads to freedom from the fear of death, which gives us the freedom to live more fully. It enables us to live in the present moment—neither anticipating the future nor regretting the past. Have the courage to do what is difficult to get the dream life you desire. It takes courage to choose the freedom to live life on your own terms.

Are you willing to go on your own Hero's journey?
For a good example of the hero's journey in the movies, think Indiana Jones. Make your life as exciting in real life as your favourite movie—perhaps with a little less physical risk. As author and professor Andrew Bernstein once said, "The hero is the man (woman) who lets no obstacle prevent him from pursuing the values he has chosen." It is our core values that keep us on course, if we don't get distracted by the demands of those with different values. Our values cry out for expression. Just as with any good story, our character develops as we work through our fears.

Action Steps – Questions to Ponder

What is your hero's journey?
Make a decision. Trust and have faith that it is the right choice for you.

What is the path you will take to reach your destination?

Which barriers will you need to overcome?

Soundtrack

"Life Is a Highway"
by Tom Cochrane

Life is a highway
I wanna ride it all night long.

Books You Might Like to Read

The Hero's Journey
by Joseph Campbell

Fire in the Belly
by Sam Keen

Also Google

Hildegard von Bingen

III.
FEAR OF POOR HEALTH

Chapter 15:
Can Thoughts Affect Your Health?

You don't always need a life-threatening disease or debilitating illness to get you started on your personal journey . . . Postponing the decision to shift gears is more than unwise; it is dangerous.

Caroline Myss

Sometimes it is hard to tell who is more stressed—those with jobs or those without. We feel stress whenever we experience prolonged negative emotions like hopelessness or anger and then do nothing about it.

We either positively create our world or we negatively create it. We need to be more conscious creators. Happiness results from both knowing who you are and expressing it.

The Philips Index (2004), National Study of Public Well-Being, reported that fewer than one in three (31 percent) of respondents believe that the world is getting better. We often sit around waiting for others—the ubiquitous "them" to make things better—be they politicians, doctors, environmentalists, and so on. I think "them" needs to be "us" more often.

The Philips Index stems from a basic insight regarding the human potential for fulfillment. "When people are happy, healthy, and open to change, they thrive by experiencing a state of well-being. There is also potential for enhanced creativity, prosperity, and satisfaction with life." There appears to be a lot of wisdom contained in a number of studies I've read that tend to sit on shelves just gathering dust. I'm glad many of them have now made it onto the Internet, but how many of us even think to look for them?

Napoleon Hill listed a number of ways the fear of ill health can manifest. Hypochondria can be a way of talking ourselves into illness. He suggested we stop focusing on the symptoms of ill health because those thoughts can make us sick. Some people go overboard using the Internet to endlessly search for symptoms. We may become more susceptible to illness due to constant worry about how to pay for future possible medical expenses. We might use alcohol or drugs to combat pains such as headaches rather than addressing the root cause.

Gabor Maté, a medical doctor who wrote the book, *When the Body Says No*, suggests *No* is a word we should use more often for the sake of our health. Risk saying No to the demands of others rather than feeling resentment after a Yes. Don't defend your actions. Ignore critics. I know that is easier said than done.

Do you believe the following statements?

1. Receiving continual criticism can result in physical illness.
2. People may treat you the way you unconsciously ask to be treated—because of the feelings you project about yourself.
3. The more you demand or crave the respect of others, the less likely you are to receive it. This is why dictators eventually get toppled.

Never blame anyone or anything else for the way you feel. That only serves to give your power away. Here's a provocative thought. Only our minds get sick; only our minds heal. Bodies don't get sick; bodies can't heal. Be careful about the words you feed your mind. What you say is what you will project. Don't say, "I am sick," if you want to be healthy. Don't say, "I am poor," if you want to be wealthy. Don't say, "I am depressed," if you want to be happy. Pain results from holding on to something that doesn't belong in our lives. In this respect, pain can be a great teacher. Focus on what you want and on the things you enjoy. Ignore what you don't want. Whatever you give priority to in your life is what you'll create.

We wear our fears like a shield of protection. Dare to proceed. Give yourself time to breathe. Risk asking for what you really want. Risk taking the lead and going out in front. This is leadership from within. It is really yourself you are leading along your own path. Others will choose their own way. We are either in command of our own lives or we are being commanded.

According to Maté, our bodies respond physically to every psychological impulse—good or bad—through our emotions. It is our emotions that cement our reactions in place. It is the fight or flight response of our caveman ancestors. Unfortunately, when the boss is guarding the entrance/exit of the cave, we start to believe we can't escape, so our flight response gets buried in our bodies and can eventually turn into disease, which also could be spelled out as dis-ease. Sometimes, illness is the only way out. We may need to replace the motto: "Do what you love, and the money will follow" with "Do what you love, and good health will follow."

Action Steps – Questions to Ponder

What is your job costing you in terms of your time, energy, and health?

Do you believe physical symptoms are the result of emotional pain?

Books You Might Like to Read

When the Body Says No
by Gabor Maté

Why People Don't Heal and How They Can
by Caroline Myss

Also Google

The Philips Index—National Study of Public Well-Being (2004)

Chapter 16:
Gross Domestic Product versus Gross National Happiness

If a man has a happy mind, he will have a happy body.

Chinese proverb

Happiness could hold the key to longevity
It seems the more enjoyment you get out of life, the longer you are likely to live. *The English Longitudinal Study of Ageing,* conducted by University College London, revealed that those who enjoy life most are three times more likely to live longer than those who don't. The research also suggested future poor health issues could be predicted by the state of a person's mind. The study tracked the psychological well-being of ten thousand people between the age of fifty and one hundred, over nine years. It concluded that happier people are less stressed, more likely to take care of themselves, and enjoy strong social ties (Banks, et al.).

The medical profession knows that stress releases glucocorticoids which can kill cells in the hippocampus. Remember the saying: Don't sweat the small stuff? That could be good advice.

What can we do to get happy?
We tend to think the answer lies in a little or a lot more money and possessions than we currently have. If money is the answer, why is it that follow-up studies on big lottery winners show they

are not happier than prior to their "big win," and sometimes are more miserable?

Science is trying to figure out what determines happiness. Is it partly due to our genetic makeup? Is some of our happiness the result of intentional activity and practiced ways of thinking and behaving? Psychologists have long known that different people can see and think about the same events in different ways.

This book is intended to change mindsets so everyone can truly enjoy his or her life and work. I'm no Pollyanna, but I recognize that happiness is a state of mind. Happiness is a habit. Upon awakening each day, choose to live happily and observe how your day unfolds. The world we live in is determined largely through what goes on inside our mind. Happy people are well–versed in the art of living well.

Is it possible that happy people are happy because they believe they deserve happiness? All your thoughts lead you back to a core belief about yourself. Be aware of any contradictory beliefs you may hold. The more happy and content people there are in the world, the better the world will be.

Expressing gratitude, kindness, and optimism can make people happier. It can't be forced, but you can make each a conscious habit. Studies have shown that the ability to savour an experience predicts happiness. Perhaps it's even better if the experiences you most enjoy are spaced apart. After all, if you were able to eat chocolate cake twenty-four hours a day, seven days a week, would this be an experience you'd savour after your ninety-ninth morsel?

If you think lots of money is the answer, consider which you would enjoy more: a seven-course meal on the best china in a posh hotel with a bottle of $750 wine and a waiter constantly at your elbow, or a picnic of French bread, cheese, fruit, and your favourite bottle of wine on the beach at sunset? Sometimes, simple pleasures really are better.

Scientific American (February 4, 2009) reported on a study that claimed *rapid thinking makes people happy*. The study's lead author, psychologist Emily Pronin, explained that our ability to think quickly can lead to elation and increased creativity. How can that be?

Have you ever watched the TV quiz show *Jeopardy* or a similar game in which you can guess answers along with the contestants? Sometimes, *Are You Smarter than a 5th Grader* is more my speed. Do you play along at home? Do you feel elated when you get the correct answer? That's exactly what Pronin is talking about.

Of course, there can also be a downside to rapid thinking. Has there ever been a time in your life when you've kept rapidly repeating thoughts like "I'm too old," "I'll never work again," "I'm too fat," or "I'm too poor." Feel free to insert you favourite refrain here. I'm certain repetition of these phrases did not make you feel happy. To combat this negative repetition, engage in activities that require you to think quickly—but also creatively. It is believed that thinking quickly unleashes the brain's novelty-loving dopamine system which is involved in the sensation of pleasure and reward. (*This may explain why I love brainstorming.*)

Another *Scientific American* article (November 24, 2010) explored the question of whether a focused mind is a happy mind. It explains that we are happiest when thought and action are aligned. Buddhists express this state as being fully present and engaged in the everyday activities of life. When you are sweeping the floor, be fully engaged in the process. When you are washing dishes, enjoy the warm soapy water and the sensual feel of each dish in your hands. It's not very relaxing to be wishing you could smash them on the sidewalk outside and be done with the task. Daydreaming about flying off to Hawaii will take you out of the present moment; it may also lead to cutting your fingers because you're not paying attention. *(This may explain why so many people have dishwashers. They can't enjoy the process of dishwashing.)*

Stop doing so many activities you find boring. Delegate them to someone who enjoys them. This will free you up to work with flow—becoming so absorbed in an activity that you are fully concentrating on it. One of the best ways to train your mind to wander less is to use a daily meditation practice.

Happiness is an attitude and a choice that is always available. Many people believe their happiness is a result of the circumstances of their lives. Other people can affect our level of happiness only if we allow them to. When we allow others to control how happy or unhappy we are, we're about as grounded as leaves in the wind. True happiness is the result of choosing to live each day in a way we have deemed worthwhile. Practice optimism. It will make you happier. Decide what you stand for and speak about it. It can be more productive than protesting what you are against. Speak up about goals that inspire you. Use your creative mind to build a better world for yourself and others.

Should GNH replace GDP?
When the King of Bhutan told the world: "The true measure of a nation's success is not the Gross Domestic Product, but Gross National Happiness," can't you just imagine our Western leaders rolling their eyes in disbelief?

Economists have long argued that the key to happiness is the attainment of more material wealth. However, Bhutan is now defying this notion. The King of Bhutan *(a landlocked state in South Asia at the eastern end of the Himalayas)* believes that true development of human society takes place when material and spiritual development take place side by side to complement and reinforce each other.

The idea of GNH is growing. The four main pillars are

1. equitable and equal socio-economic development
2. preservation and promotion of cultural and spiritual heritage
3. conservation of the environment

4. good governance at both national and local levels, which is both complementary and consistent

Prosperity is defined in more enhanced terms by measuring how happy people are rather than measuring what they consume. This has resulted in Bhutan becoming more self-sufficient and self-reliant, reducing the gap between rich and poor and empowering her people.

The American Association of Retired Persons (AARP) implemented a research project (Beyond Happiness: Thriving 2012) to uncover what happiness and well-being mean to middle-aged and older Americans. They discovered that happiness levels are on the decline due to the economy, with those in their early fifties experiencing the lowest point of well-being.

Good health and strong relationships tied for the two highest dimensions for happiness. Meaning and accomplishment ranked second. Money was rated lowest, except for those with less than $25,000 a year in income.

Most respondents believed they were at least partially in control of their own happiness and thought control over happiness increased with age as they became more interested in enjoying the everyday simple pleasures of life.

Those aged fifty to eighty said some of the activities that contributed to their happiness included enjoying nature, engaging in a spiritual practice, music, travel, spending time with pets, overcoming a challenge, achieving personal goals, being absorbed in a hobby or interest, being immersed in a book or completing a word puzzle. Activities rooted in gratitude and kindness topped the list.

Following an international seminar on Gross National Happiness, held in Bhutan in 2004, participants established a *Gross International Happiness Index*. Three of the participants you might want to read about include *Corptools / Values Centre* in the United States, *Genuine Progress Indicators / GPI* Atlantic in

Canada, and The *New Economics Foundation* in the United Kingdom.

Helena Norberg-Hodge wrote "Towards an Economics of Happiness" in the Summer 2012 edition of the *RSF Quarterly*. She explained that prior to the Industrial Revolution, people were more likely to work together in a community. Think of the children's rhyme, Rub-a-Dub-Dub, about the butcher, the baker, the candlestick maker, and you'll know what she means. I'm not sure why the farmers weren't included in this rhyme. I'm sure most of us wouldn't be here without them. At that time, people were dependent on each other for survival. They bought locally. This is how communities grew and thrived; they traded their products and services with each other. They weren't searching the Internet for the best deal in town.

I believe our future physical and psychological security depends on a return to a version of this model—especially when it comes to our food. It may even help to revive our downtown small-scale retail stores.

Norberg-Hodge encourages small-scale, diversified food production as a way to build skills and provide employment along with fresh, tasty food with cheaper delivery costs. It's heartening to read that youth are forming a growing back-to-the-land movement—exchanging computers for hoes.

I've read about a number of small-scale food production methods on the trend-watching website, Springwise. We can grow a variety of produce in a small outdoor plot of land, on a balcony, or even inside an apartment. There is a movement toward Vertical Gardening as a method to grow a lot of our own food in a condensed space. Gardening and meal preparation are basic skills anyone can learn. If you are unable to participate in growing your own food, choose to support your local farmers market. People who enjoy their work produce the best products.

Other ways to get happy
Have you been humming a song lately that sounds a lot like

Peggy Lee's top hit, "Is That All There Is?" If so, you'll want to know that breaking out the booze to drown your sorrows is unlikely to bring lasting happiness.

Researchers from the relatively new field of Positive Psychology have begun to explore what makes people happy. Over the past century, our culture has emphasized buying our happiness through acquiring more goods and services. When the economy drops and we lose our jobs, along with our purchasing power, we need to find our happiness elsewhere. This may be one reason for our increased focus on spirituality.

One of the key findings on what produces happiness is a feeling of gratitude for what we currently have. Close friendships and strong family ties create not only a sense of belonging, but also provide us with a community we can have fun with who can also offer practical support. There's nothing inherently wrong with money or material goods—they just don't tend to give life meaning.

Remember what Maslow said about self-actualization?
Most Boomers will be familiar with Abraham Maslow's "Hierarchy of Needs." He described self-actualized people as those who fulfill their potential by doing everything they are capable of. They strive to find meaning in a life that is important to them. He believed only one in a hundred people will achieve it (Maslow, 1968; McLeod, 2007). I'd like to increase those odds. After our basic needs for food, safety, and shelter are met, we are free to seek knowledge, personal growth, and a way to help others. What often trips us up is our fear.

We stay in jobs or relationships we dislike because we're afraid of change. We are often held back by our fears of what others might think. To become self-actualized, you must transcend these fears. Great careers will give you a chance to express your unique talents and abilities. If you choose your work based solely on which career will pay the most, the price you'll likely pay is your unexplored dreams. Bookshelves are filled with stories of people who sold their souls for too high a price, e.g., Robin Sharma's *The Monk Who Sold His Ferrari.*

Maslow identified Abraham Lincoln and Albert Einstein as two of the people he considered self-actualized. He listed fifteen characteristics representative of a self-actualized person.

Maslow's Characteristics of a Self-actualized Person

Maslow would describe you as self-actualized if you

- tolerate uncertainty
- accept yourself and others for who they are
- act with spontaneity
- focus on solving problems
- have a sense of humour
- look at life objectively
- exhibit creativity
- resist enculturation
- show concern for the welfare of humanity
- have a deep appreciation of life
- maintain satisfying relationships with a few people
- need privacy
- behave in a democratic manner
- have strong ethics

Maslow identified behaviour that leads to Self-actualization

Maslow said you are likely self-actualized if you

- experience life like a child does
- try new things willingly
- listen to your feelings
- act with honesty and without pretense
- are willing to be unpopular
- take responsibility and work hard
- have the courage to give up your defenses

Humanistic psychology focuses on personal fulfillment and self-actualization. It suggests life is an on-going process of choosing either safety or growth. If we are only working to satisfy our need for safety, while disliking our job, we need to make a conscious choice to move on so that we can grow in the process. So, be honest with yourself. Take responsibility for your own happiness. Be prepared to be unpopular. Be yourself—not a clone. Experience life fully. Let your experiences fully absorb you. Live in the present moment. Use your intelligence. Express yourself. Maximize your potential. Know thyself! It's the key to self-actualization.

Happiness can only be lived in the present moment. Cultivate happiness in yourself and share it with others. Be joyful in both the giving and receiving of gifts. Give for the pleasure in giving. Expect nothing in return. Cultivate your inner child. People with childlike attitudes tend to have the most powerful experiences.

What makes me happy is recognizing there is an incredible amount of good work in progress. Thanks to the Internet, it is easy to locate. Good thing, as the dominant media is providing little coverage. Do a word search for Social Enterprise and you will see for yourself. If you are beginning to doubt that a change for the better is possible, have a look at Architects of Change on Knowledge Network. It's also available online.

Action Steps – Questions to Ponder

What do you derive the most happiness from?

Are you happy with your work?

Books You Might Like to Read

The Happiness Project
by Gretchen Rubin

The Small-Mart Revolution
by Michael H. Shuman

Ripples from the Zambezi
by Ernesto Sirolli

Also Google

Do Something Different
The premise of this site is that if you can change your habits, you can stay young longer. To be happy in life, you need to be flexible in your behaviour. That's why it is important to do something different.

www.theeconomicsofhappiness.org

www.PsycheTruth.net

www.simplypsychology.org/maslow.html

www.thrivemovement.com

Chapter 17:
Do You Have Work-Life Balance?

What shall we think of a well-adjusted slave? Culture itself is an adaptive tool . . . The more evolved and psychologically healthy people get, the more will enlightened management policy be necessary in order to survive in competition, and the more handicapped will be an enterprise with an authoritarian policy.

Abraham Maslow

When working isn't working for you
In 1974, Studs Terkel's book, *Working*, was popular reading. It documented the thoughts of dozens of people who were looking for both income and meaning from their work. Most of us still want that. Although modern technology has enabled us to become more productive—our satisfaction with work appears to have decreased.

Terkel said, "Most of us have jobs that are too small for our spirits." His interviews with workers from all walks of life revealed that people wanted their jobs to be as fulfilling as their free time.

Of course, work need not define us, but it often does.

A more recent book, written in a similar format, is *What Should I Do with My Life?* by Po Bronson. He says that "we are all writing the story of our life . . . we want to ensure that when the ending comes . . . we will not have squandered our time here." His book details the stories of people who were honest with themselves, found their own voice, and then took action to create fulfilling lives based on their dreams.

Bronson believes what I believe, that the future of work belongs to those who find their passion and work with it. The most productive workers are those who work with passion—whether it's for themselves or as an employee. This is how economic growth will and should thrive—when people are working at what they passionately believe in.

What the research shows

Working on your own terms can improve your health. Research shows that stress is the cause of many mental and physical health problems. Both Canadian and American Baby Boomers are reporting increased stress on the job, as Canadian and American studies show stress at work is on the rise. Workers are increasingly suffering from burnout. Increased stress has resulted in higher levels of worker absenteeism and illness.

In his book, *When the Body Says No*, Dr. Gabor Maté tells us that when people feel a sense of control over both their work and their lives, they experience better health. He cites a study in which employees had a higher risk of heart disease than their managers even though their incomes were almost identical. The difference between the two groups was that the managers had more power and control over their lives.

Maté cites stress researcher Dr. Hans Selye who points out that the most important stressors are emotional. Researchers have identified three factors that universally lead to stress: uncertainty, lack of information, and lack of control. All three are present in the lives of individuals with chronic conditions.

Selye also explains that sometimes people find themselves in situations where they feel trapped and unable to escape. If they are not attuned to what their emotions are trying to tell them and don't seek a way out, stress can negatively affect their health. This may be what Anais Nin was referring to when she wrote "when one is pretending, the entire body revolts."

Helplessness, real or perceived, is a potent trigger for biological stress responses. Maté asserts that learned helplessness is exemplified by "someone who feels stuck in an abusive relationship, in a stressful job or in a lifestyle that robs him or her of true freedom."

Recognize how empowering it is to be able to affect change in your own life—to be able to choose your own future rather than cater to the whims of others. Don't waste your time and energy fighting existing models of work under the old-school system of hierarchy. Instead, create a new model that will best serve you.

Many of my clients have complained about difficult employers to work for. I've had my own share of "problem" bosses. What we need to remember is that we can't change anyone else. We can only change ourselves. Employers suffer from the same fears as the rest of us. If you are working for an unhappy employer, odds are, you aren't happy either. It is usually the employer's management style that sets the tone of the workplace. It's also hard to live someone else's dream.

Work on your own fears. Decide what you want in a workplace—then you'll know when you find it. Working as a free agent can empower us all. From that strength, we can then collaborate and work with others as equals. Hierarchy no longer works for us. I'm not sure it ever did.

The elusive Work-Life balance
In 2001, Linda Duxbury and Chris Higgins produced a discussion paper on work-life balance for Health Canada. The study revealed that work-life conflict has steadily increased due to more job insecurity and heavier work demands. This includes working more hours per week due to advances in technology that allow workers to be on call twenty-four hours a day, seven days a week.

They discovered that "workers have become more stressed, physical and mental health has declined, and so has satisfaction with life . . . on the whole, jobs have become more stressful and less satisfying."Some of the twenty-seven recommendations from the report include the need to give employees increased control and flexibility regarding when and where they work. This includes opportunities for part-time work, increased personal leave days *(without justification)*, and meaningful employee participation in decision-making with improved information-sharing between management and employees.

What knowledge workers expect is a greater "democratization" of the workplace—a say in decisions affecting their jobs and employment. They are seeking a career—not just a "job"—and they want a meaningful life outside of work. Both younger and older workers also want the ability to work flexible hours (Duxbury & Higgins, 2001).

The report references Graham S. Lowe's book *The Quality of Work*. A key point Lowe makes is that although the past few decades have produced lots of popular business books, management training and theories that extol the importance of human resources, recognition of employees as the key to business is a hollow reality.

The key finding of the report was that the more control employees felt they had over their lives, the more they were able to balance work and family. Employees who had flexibility concerning when and where they worked, a supportive work environment, autonomy, a sense of empowerment, good two-way communication between employer and employee, a realistic workload, and self-directed work teams were the most satisfied with their work-life balance.

Interestingly, they discovered that those who perceive less control and more stress tend to buy more goods and services. This can become a vicious circle where you use "shopping therapy" to quell your pain and need to keep your job to pay your bills.

I can attest to this. Whenever I've had a job I didn't enjoy, I would shop until I dropped—often dropping half my paycheque at the Eaton's Centre during my lunch hour.

A follow-up study by Duxbury and Higgins in 2003 entitled, *Work-Life Conflict in Canada in the New Millennium,* revealed employees are saying they want to leave stressful workplaces so they can regain control over their own time. Many want to have more input into scheduling their work hours as they are yearning for work-life balance. They lament that employers are unwilling to relinquish control. Results of this study are summarized on the Human Resources Service Development Canada website (Duxbury & Higgins, 2003).

Another study, Under *Pressure—Implications of Work-Life Balance and Job Stress,* a Human Solutions™ Report, found that 30 percent of employees report that their job is the source of a large amount of the stress they experience (Lowe, 2006).

The link between job stress and health has overburdened Canada's health care system. Twice, I have worked in offices *(with thirty to fifty employees)* in which more than one-fifth of the staff have gone off on long-term sick leave. Can we deny a connection between stress and health?

Work-related stress is so pervasive that if employers are unable to address it, workers will. I believe this is part of Generation Y's mantra. They've seen what jobs have done to their parents and want no part of it.

Canada introduced standards for mental health in the workplace
In January 2013, the Mental Health Association of Canada released a report entitled *Psychological Health and Safety in the Workplace*. The guidance document aims to persuade employers to voluntarily pledge to reduce stress in the workplace, help employees achieve work-life balance, treat employees with respect and appreciation, and to recognize that happy employees are healthy employees—both physically and mentally (CSA Group, 2013; Gordon, 2013).

Many workers will not want to wait for these to become common practice.

Americans don't have Work-Life balance either
Work-Life balance is also off-kilter in the United States. According to a 2010 survey by Bradley Honan of *Strategy One,* of the 89 percent of Americans who said work-life balance was a problem, 54 percent felt the problem was significant, while 43 percent believed their employer was not doing enough to address the problem (Gurchiek, 2010; PR Newswire, 2010).

The Society for Human Resource Management participated in a White House Forum on workplace flexibility in 2010. The President's Council of Economic Advisors released a report, *Work-Life Balance and the Economics of Workplace Flexibility,* in conjunction with the forum (Council of Economic Advisors, 2010; Rouse, 2010).

Most significant was that the findings were almost identical to the Canadian reports. Workers want greater control over their time so they can achieve work-life balance. A further conclusion was that if this were achieved, it could lead to greater productivity and improved morale, with the spin-off effect of an improved economy. This makes sense. How productive can employees be if they are at work wishing they were somewhere else?

Does anyone read these reports?
A 2011 survey by the American Psychological Association found that many U. S. workers feel stressed-out and undervalued. Only 54 percent said their organization made them feel valued, 28 percent intend to seek new employment, 41 percent feel stressed at work, and 32 percent have difficulty with work-life balance (American Psychological Association, 2011).

The report *Work-Life Balance in the New Millennium* (2001) concludes with the statement: "All that is required is a shift in attitude" (Duxbury & Higgins, 2001). Not much has changed since David J. Schwartz wrote his book, *The Magic of Getting What You Want,* in 1983. In it he concluded that "aggressive union activity, personnel turnover, absenteeism, and related problems are due to a lack of respect by managers for their employees." I think a huge shift in attitude is long overdue.

My belief is that it is better not to wait for employers to change their minds or attitudes. It's easier to change our own. If we can't find work that supports our needs with an existing employer, we'll need to create our own employment. Hierarchies tend to favour and promote one group of people over another. I believe the days of top-down management are numbered, thanks in large part to Gen Y and social networking. Recognize that there is such a thing as healthy anger. It can help you reclaim your voice and project your own values, beliefs, and ideas. Speak up. Use your anger constructively to help improve conditions for the world. Focus on what you are for, rather than what you are against.

Remember the lines from Shakespeare: "This above all: to thine own self be true. And it must follow as the night the day, thou canst not then be false to any man."

Ways to get stress under control
Dr. Andrew Weil, author of *Healthy Aging*, recommends we minimize our level of stress over the long-term because otherwise it will age us. This is because the stress hormone, cortisol, is toxic to nerve cells in areas of the brain concerned with memory and emotion. He suggests using breath work as a means of controlling our unwanted stress. Meditation and yoga are two approaches. Regular practice may also give you a glimpse of the spiritual side of yourself. It provides both the time and space to pose questions about who you are and what your purpose is and then to pause, breathe, and listen for the answers.

In Nancy Anderson's book, *Work with Passion in Midlife & Beyond*, she references Dr. John E. Sarno, author of *Healing Back Pain: The Mind-Body Connection*. Dr. Sarno believes "the health care industry consumes billions of dollars every year treating the physical symptoms of emotional pain."

The media regularly reports that Boomers are likely to leave their full-time jobs and work either freelance or as entrepreneurs. Casey Dowd reflects what many believe when she says Boomers "still want to work, just on their own terms," in her FoxBusiness article (Dowd, 2012). I'm guessing this will also lead to improved health because people will have time to eat better, sleep longer, socialize more often with family and friends, pursue recreational activities and have less need to dull their pain with mindless shopping.

Anyone who has ever laughed at a Dilbert comic *(the comic strip focuses on life in office cubicle hell)* or watched the TV show, *The Office,* and then gulped when they recognized themselves in the process, can probably relate to the prediction Scott Adams made in his book, *The Dilbert Future.* Adams predicted that skilled workers would soon be trading in their jobs for self-employment, in record numbers. I wonder if his comic strip influenced many people to do that.

How the Dalai Lama is enhancing science

The Dalai Lama is working on the leading edge of science—in conjunction with neuroscientists. Cutting-edge neuroscience is joining forces with the ancient wisdom of Buddhism to show how we have the power to change our brains by changing our minds. Personal transformation is within reach for all of us (Haven, 2010; Hamilton, 2005).

Scientists are using brain imaging to study the brains of Buddhist monks and their practice of *mindfulness.* An important component of changing the brain is to tap into the power of the mind through focused attention which is achieved during meditation. Meditation is mind-training to help you perceive the world in a different, more positive way. It cultivates an inner calmness.

What the research is showing is that we cannot only alter the structure of our brains, but we can also generate new neurons. New neurons are created in the brain every day, even into old age. Meditation can also affect the telomeres (the tips of chromosomes)—slowing down the aging process. *(The telemeres in our brain shorten throughout life. Once they are gone, so are we.)*

Shalini Bahl teaches a webinar on Mindfulness at Work. She says with so much multi-tasking going on, we've lost our ability to remain focused. Studies reveal that our minds are wandering half the time we are awake. If you've witnessed drivers behind the wheel putting on makeup or talking on a cellphone, you'll agree with her.

Mindfulness training is a growing industry, commonly associated with sitting meditation. Apple and Google are two companies that have implemented the training into the workplace. Scientific research at Harvard Medical School has revealed through brain scans that neural pathways are altered by mindfulness and can create new ways of responding to familiar emotional triggers, reducing typical knee-jerk reactions.

It is also possible to reset our happiness meter. Evidently, we come with a happiness meter in our original DNA. We now know genuine happiness cannot be fulfilled through the outer world alone and that our state of mind can override our outer conditions. (Viktor Frankl wrote about this in *Man's Search for Meaning*.)

The Dalai Lama became involved in this neuroscience project because the research implies we can learn and teach loving kindness and compassion which is a key step in creating a more peaceful world. We underestimate the power of our minds to transform ourselves. The implication is that by changing our minds, we can change the world.

I have experienced the power of intense loving kindness twice in my life. The first time was during the Papal visit to the Martyr's Shrine in Midland, Ontario, where I was a volunteer. Although I am not Catholic, I felt intense love emanating from Pope John Paul. The second time was during an interview with an eighty-year-old Buddhist monk while I was conducting a survey for Tourism Vancouver Island. The incredible love and compassion emanating from this man was very powerful, even though we were merely discussing tourism. I was so disappointed when he had to board his plane and our conversation ended.

For the past eighteen months, I have meditated for fifteen minutes every day. When my job came to an abrupt end last year, I was unusually calm about it. I wonder if that was partially due to my meditation practice.

Action Steps – Questions to Ponder

Do you currently experience work-life balance?

Calculate the number of days you or your co-workers missed work due to stress or illness.

Do you believe happy people are healthier?

Would you like more flexibility on the job?

How would you define flexibility on the job for yourself?

How can you reduce stress in your life?

Do you meditate? Would you like to try?

Soundtrack

from the movie *Nine to Five*

"Working Nine to Five"
Dolly Parton

Working nine to five
What a way to make a living.

Books You Might Like to Read

Working
by Studs Terkel

What Should I Do With My Life?
by Po Bronson

The Quality of Work
by Graham S. Lowe

Healthy Aging
by Dr. Andrew Weil

The Dilbert Future
by Scott Adams

Also Google

Discussion Paper on Work-Life Balance
by Linda Duxbury & Chris Higgins

Work-Life Conflict in Canada in the New Millenium
by Linda Duxbury & Chris Higgins

Under Pressure – Implications of Work-Life Balance and Job Stress
A Human Solutions™ Report (2006)

Work-Life Balance and the Economics of Workplace Flexibility
The President's Council of Economic Advisors

Older Workers in the Labour Market

2010 survey by Bradley Honan of Strategy One

2011 survey by the American Psychological Association

Psychological health and safety in the workplace (2013)
Commissioned by the Mental Health Association of Canada

Mindfulness at Work
webinar by Shalini Bahl

You might be familiar with the popular TV show, *The Dog Whisperer,* featuring Cesar Milan. Here's an interesting observation he has made:

Humans are the only species who follow unstable leaders.

Cesar Milan

IV.
FEAR OF LOSS OF LOVE

Chapter 18:
Our Work Is Love Made Visible

There is a candle in your heart, ready to be kindled.
There is a void in your soul, ready to be filled.
You feel it, don't you?

Rumi

When the power of love overcomes the love of power,
the world will know peace.

Jimi Hendrix

Our culture has largely separated our passion from our work. In midlife we feel an urge to re-align our gifts and passion with the needs of the world. It is through our work that we are best able to evolve ourselves. It is who we become while we are on this journey that is our goal. Our work can be our best expression of our love made visible.

Our Work is not driven by the pursuit of wealth, although money can be a by-product. It is driven more by our desire for self-expression and meaning. It is how we make sense of our place in the world.

What's your calling?
Are you being called to grow in a way that best taps into your passion and inborn gifts—and perhaps your vulnerability? What

makes you unique? Can you see patterns in your life that weave together your personal story? What work can you do that will enable you to remove the mask that shields your real self from the world?

Rather than searching for whom to love, can you focus on what you love doing? That will connect you with others on a similar path. This will help you find what you have to give back to society. Who wants a leader, doctor, carpenter, or career counsellor who is unable to follow her own heart and love her work?

Low self-worth is a primary cause of self-sabotage. Realizing your innate self-worth expands your horizon and opens up possibilities. Maturana wrote that "love is the one emotion that expands intelligence because love connects us." Only by expressing self-love can we truly love another.

Own your power to create the work you love. Seize it for yourself because it will not be handed to you on a silver platter. It is the ultimate act of self-love and is a pre-requisite to sharing your loving work with others. It is akin to an airline's admonition for parents to don their own oxygen mask first before they give their children oxygen.

When work becomes your calling, there's no telling where that path will lead you. That's what makes it so exciting.

Action Steps

What major challenges have you triumphed over?

What lessons did you learn?

What knowledge from these challenges can you share with others?

What are your thoughts on this quote?

*If each of us did nothing more than
to take responsibility for ourselves,
none of us would have to wish that
we could change the word.*

Shad Helmstetter

A Book You Might Like to Read

The Consultant's Calling
by Geoffrey M. Bellman

Chapter 19:
You Get What You Give

Work is love made visible. And if you cannot work with love but only with distaste, it is better that you should leave your work and sit at the gate of the temple and take alms from those who work with joy.

Kahil Gibran

As we look ahead into the next century, leaders will be those who empower others.

Bill Gates

To lead people, walk behind them.

Lao Tzu

Sakyong Mipham, a lama from Tibet, wrote in *Ruling Your World*, "Caring for others is the basis of worldly success. This is the secret that we don't learn in school."

We need to recognize our interdependence with others in the circle of life. We are part of something larger than ourselves. Whenever we feel disconnected and alone, it shuts us down. We need to be able to both give and receive. Each of us has a role to play. Our actions create ripples that touch others. As with the one hundredth monkey syndrome, recognize your connection to all humanity. When we connect with others through service, it provides both meaning and purpose in our lives. Service is a relationship between equals. Whatever we give, we receive.

Servant leadership, defined in 1970 by Robert Greenleaf, founder of the modern servant leadership movement, is a practical philosophy. Servant leaders serve others in alignment with their values and integrity. Instead of top-down hierarchy, servant leaders emphasize collaboration, active listening, trust, teamwork, empathy, and the ethical use of power. It nourishes people and encourages different perspectives and evokes the best qualities in everyone (Smith, 2005).

This is the type of leadership we need and I encourage Boomers to take the lead. We can't wait for government or large companies to do this for us. We can identify the most important issues in our local communities and then develop strategies to make change happen. There are excellent examples of this in my own community. One group of Boomers has created The Gabriola Commons and a second group fundraised and organized the building of a local Health Care Centre.

The work of Peter Senge has greatly influenced me. His knowledge of systems theory played a major role in my Master's program. In conjunction with others, Senge wrote the book, *Presence*, which brought together ideas I've pondered for decades—ideas that have caused me to think deeply about my life. A passage in Presence states, "The ultimate aim of the servant leader, the quest, is to find the resources of character to meet your destiny, and to find the wisdom and power to serve life that way . . . we have no idea of our capacity to create the world anew." I hope this quote will also influence your life.

Mankind is at the heart of our economic system. Bruce Lipton has pointed out that it is our own behaviour that has been destroying our planet and ourselves, and it is up to us to reverse this trend. No one else can save us.

Your Life Purpose
I believe the purpose of life is to serve one another through the use of our inborn gifts. As our gifts differ, we are interdependent—so we trade our products and services with each other. Our "middleman" is money—although barter is another medium of

exchange. I'm convinced we remain in touch with God / Oneness / Our Higher Power both before our birth and after our death. The way we express this connection is through our inherent gifts.

In *Money and the Meaning of Life*, Jacob Needleman suggests money is the medium that links man's spiritual needs with his material needs. He tells us the original coins represented this link between both worlds—by having a sacred symbol (God) on one side and a secular symbol (Caesar) on the other. He also reminds us that in ancient Greece, Hermes was both the god of commerce and the god of communication between man and the immortals. The expression "do what you love (spiritual realm), and the money (material realm) will follow," demonstrates the connection between these worlds.

To *do what you love* first requires you to *know yourself*. That is also why seeking money first for its own sake fails to satisfy. So, who are you, and what do you really want to do with your life? Get conscious with your search. I'd love to replace the job postings on Employment Centre job boards with a big mirror around which are the words, "Once you know yourself, you will find your work."

Our gifts—like art that arrives through a muse—are gifts from the Divine. If it sells in the marketplace, it can provide an income. If it doesn't, it is still a gift you can share with the world. You will simply need to use another of your gifts to provide an income. Don't let the money issue hold you back.

Needleham tells us that money can buy us everything except meaning. We must discover that for ourselves. Keep in mind that money itself has no value until it is spent in exchange for someone else's goods or services. There is nothing inherently wrong with money. It is merely a form of energy, and like all energy, the important part is how we spend it. Recall Mother Theresa's admonition that "sometimes we hunger for more than bread."

Spiritual Leaders of our Time

Ironically, I see Warren Buffet as one of the great spiritual leaders of our time. I expected to give the Dalai Lama top billing under this heading, but I think it is Buffet who speaks a language more people are seeking to comprehend. He is a billionaire who does not worship money. He has money because he enjoys using his gifts to serve the world. He has given most of his money away and has been content to live a modest life. He epitomizes the ability to follow both the spiritual and material paths. Oprah is another good role model. You might prefer to follow her lead as she not only enjoys what she has, but she also is willing to share both her wealth and herself with the world.

Service can be an act of self-transcendence if we do it without regard to self-interest. How we serve can be the key to a meaningful life that connects us to our world and each other.

I've read that Social Enterprise is now the largest class at Harvard University. A social enterprise is an organization that applies market-based strategies to maximize improvements in human and environmental well-being, rather than maximizing profit for external shareholders. How's that for a change for the better? Social entrepreneurship may be the best way to change the world.

Action Steps – Questions to Ponder

Do you love your life and your work?

What are you passionate about?

What is your motivation for working in midlife?

Is your work in alignment with your core values?

Ask yourself: How can I best serve the world?
Your contribution to the world will be through your strengths.

Soundtrack

from the movie *Alfie*

"What's It All About, Alfie?"
Cilla Black with Burt Bacharach

Are we meant to take more than we give?

Books You Might Like to Read

Presence
by Peter Senge and Others

Leadership from Within
by Peter Urs Bender

Also Google

Social Enterprise
Servant Leadership
Dragon Dreaming
Ashoka
Architects of Change
(A program on the Knowledge Network.)

Chapter 20:
Does Maslow Have The Answer?

A musician must make music, an artist must paint, a poet must write, if he is to ultimately be at peace with himself . . . What a man can be, he must be. This need we call self-actualization.

Abraham Maslow

There are three things extremely hard:
steel, a diamond, and to know one's self.

Benjamin Franklin

Wayne Dyer's mentor, Abraham Maslow, identified three characteristics of self-actualizing people: (1) They are independent of the good opinion of others. They think for themselves. (2) They are detached from outcome. They are focused on what they give, not on what they will receive. (3) They have no desire to have power or control over others (Maw, 2012).

Self-actualized people fulfill their potential. They accept themselves and others as they are and enjoy problem-solving to help others improve their own lives. They have a strong sense of personal ethics and responsibility. Their career choices reflect their genuine personal values and ideals.

I believe that when you are no longer able to maximize your talents on the job, it's time to move on. Instead of focusing your energy on what you can get, focus on what you can give. Both people and things constantly flow in and out of our lives. Allow them to flow freely. Try not to hold on too tightly. Don't waste time comparing yourself with others or trying to climb above them. Ask how you can best serve. Then, rise to the challenge.

Viktor Frankl, author of *Man's Search for Meaning*, believed a lack of meaning in a person's life causes the most stress. He is thought to have coined the term "Sunday neurosis"—referring to a form of anxiety resulting from an awareness in some people of the emptiness of their lives once the weekend is over. Is this why most heart attacks happen on Monday mornings?

Frankl believed it is our responsibility to create meaning in our lives. He viewed suffering not as an obstacle to happiness but often as a necessary path. If we can find work that relieves the suffering of others, that can lead to our own happiness.

He suggested America erect a "Statue of Responsibility" on the West Coast to counterbalance the Statue of Liberty on the East Coast. The project is still in progress. It symbolizes the responsibility that comes with liberty.

In high school, Plato's *Republic* was required reading in my English class. I've always remembered the Allegory of the Cave. There are many YouTube explanations available. I think an easier explanation might be to watch the Wizard of Oz. It provides a good understanding of the way we live with illusions. Fortunately, we are able to look behind the curtain and see the truth whenever we choose. (*I Googled the two together, and it turns out others agree with me on this connection.*) Are there any illusions you might be living with? Are you afraid to walk out of your self-imposed cave? Hopefully, you do not believe that ignorance is bliss.

Over the years, I've noticed that those who complained the most about their workplaces were often the least likely to leave and look for another line of work. I remember more than one co-worker telling me she wouldn't leave because it was "only thirteen more years until retirement with a full pension." Yikes! Even a gold-plated cave is still a cave. Move towards the light!

I believe we have found our work when we are engaged both heart and soul, and it challenges us to grow. If you feel compelled to perform your work even in the face of criticism, and there is nothing else you would rather be doing, you have found your passion. Our true work is a gift we give ourselves. It has the power to completely transform us.

Action Steps – Questions to Ponder

Do you think Viktor Frankl is right when he says with freedom comes responsibility?

Are there any illusions you might be living with?

Are you afraid to walk out of your self-imposed cave?

What is one thing you can do to start expressing more of who you are?

Soundtrack 🎵

from *The Wizard of Oz*
"We're off to See the Wizard"

A Book You Might Like to Read

The Power of Intention
by Dr. Wayne Dyer

Chapter 21:
Yes—You Are Creative!

The primary responsibility of our lives is to be creative.

Freeman Patterson

Imagination is more important than knowledge. Imagination is everything. It is the preview of life's coming attractions.

Albert Einstein

Most people die before they are fully born. Creativeness means to be born before one dies.

Erich Fromm

We are all born creative. Our subconscious mind is the seat of our emotions and is our creative mind. Once our subconscious mind accepts an idea, it begins to execute it. We just need to be open to allowing our creativity to emerge and flow in a positive manner. Always focus on what you want rather than on what you don't want. Your thoughts are creative in that they create whatever you think about, whether it is good or bad. If you think the world is filled with misery, you will see that. If you think it is filled with beauty, you will see beauty.

If someone else dictates how our work is to be performed, the work is no longer a creative art. It might be a paint-by-number, but how long would that format satisfy you? To fully express your creativity, you must own the work process. I can no more deliver someone else's workshops in an "artful manner" than another comedian can artfully deliver jokes written for Jerry Seinfeld. You need to design your own work for it to ring true.

As the demand for customized products and services increases, cookie-cutter solutions will decrease. Our work is to provide the solutions people are looking for. Design your work to match your own skills and interests. It was Don Marquis, journalist and author, who said, "Ours is a world where people don't know what they want and are willing to go through hell to get it." If you are currently going through hell, please concentrate on finding a way out.

Dick Richards, author of *Artful Work*, explained how the mechanization of the industrial age resulted in production of identical assembly-line products, removing the opportunity for workers to inject their own creativity into the process. Prior to this era, artisans made individual products that directly served the needs of their customers. In most cases, buyer and seller would meet face-to-face.

The advent of mechanization somehow came to mandate a group of people who didn't actually produce anything—they merely made sure other people did the work. This was the rise of management, hierarchy, and bureaucracy.

Thanks to our increasingly wired (or wireless) world, the playing field is being leveled. Workers are wising up to the fact that people who manage the process of goods and services are not more deserving than those who actually do the work. Professional knowledge-based workers, in particular, are fleeing top-heavy organizations for "free agent" options that enable them to do their work in a more creative manner while self-managing the process. It is difficult to serve two masters. Do you wish to serve the needs of your boss or your clients/customers? People are increasingly choosing to follow where their own integrity leads.

Government and Unions don't have the answer

The disappearance of jobs is a huge social issue. Elections are often won and lost on it. Job loss has created anxiety, anger, and confusion in many of us. Although we need work, it need not be pre-packaged in a job format. Government seems incapable of leading us toward a better economic future. Instead, they feed the fear-mongering machine to get elected. That's not leadership. It is self-serving manipulation. We need leadership that will show us how to lead ourselves to a better future.

I'm hoping this book encourages you to seek out that kind of leadership for yourself. We are all in this together. In serving each other's needs, we can also serve our own need for self-expression. That's the type of co-operative work style I'm looking for—to replace the dog-eat-dog mentality with a conscious desire to serve each other. What you might be good at is not the same as what I am good at—so we can trade with each other. Too bad political parties can't do likewise.

Let's kill some sacred cows

Government is telling us we need to manage our own careers, but they are not showing us how to do so. School systems trained us for industrial-age work, in which most of our jobs are directed by others. Once we're thrown out the door, we're told to figure out on our own how to market our skills and take control of our own futures. No wonder people are confused. Unions are still out striking for "job security." Hello! That's going the way of the Dodo bird. Teach workers the skills they need for portable employment instead.

Government-funded employment services are primarily directed toward training people for a traditional job search for jobs that no longer exist. They continue to teach how to write a resumé, a cover letter, and practice interview questions.

There's no point teaching that networking is the best way to find work *(which it is)*, if people have skipped the work they need to do within themselves. What is inside you that needs to be expressed in your work? Until you know this, how will you know what you are networking about? What value do you offer? Which skills do you want to use? Once you fully understand what you have to offer that fulfills the needs of others, it will be fairly straightforward to compose a resumé or cover letter, if you think you need one. A broadcast letter or marketing plan might serve you better.

We've been brainwashed in this now outmoded manner of job search for so long that we've come to think the only way to work is to go out begging for a job. Have you ever gone out on Halloween night and returned home with a bag of your neighbour's old Christmas candy? Do you want your future work to be a trick or a treat? Some of the job postings out there have sucker written all over them.

Many clients are convinced a job is the only way to work and panic when their "dream job" fails to manifest. Employment counsellors often have no better idea "where the jobs are," than you do. Once unemployed, they can be just as lost. They are also feeling a lot of stress due to the bureaucracy that is being downloaded onto their shoulders.

Why are we continuing to teach people how to look for work in the "old economy" rather than in the "new world" economy? By printing job postings and placing them in a prominent display called a job board, we are giving job seekers a holy shrine to worship at. And they do— sometimes—for months on end. It is a false god they are idolizing. This is a dangerous game to play with a vulnerable audience desperate to find work. There has to be a better way to guide people. We need to tell them to look inside themselves for the answers.

We need to teach how to view ourselves as a business of one and then to self-market our skills in the most appropriate manner. Reclaim your dignity. Sell your best skills to those who really need them. There is ALWAYS work that needs to be done. It doesn't have to come pre-packaged in a job format. In fact, you'll enjoy it more if you can customize it to match your own skills and mission to serve.

Yes - You Are Creative!

Reclaim your authentic voice
We need to reclaim ownership and control of not only our work processes, but of our careers. If we don't do this in midlife, we never will, and we will die before our authentic voice is ever heard. Reclaim your power. Own it. Express it in your work. Refuse to be silenced any longer. In creating and expressing your work, you are developing yourself. Give voice to what needs to be expressed through you. Find your missing pieces. Bring your whole soul into your work. Work can be our ultimate form of self-expression. That is what makes it artful— it is infused with the soul of its creator. Own who you are and what your soul wants for you.

What's your purpose? Why are you here? That's your artful work. Once you are aware of your purpose, you will be able to figure out how to achieve it. Don't wait for divine inspiration to hand it to you on a silver platter. Hopefully, this book is starting to point you in the right direction.

It is through our work that we can contribute something of value toward making the world a better place. Midlife is likely our last chance to do what we love and to make a conscious contribution. More and more Boomers are seizing this opportunity to do so. They are finding an environment that nurtures their soul and moving there.

One of the Boomers I interviewed for my M.A. thesis, B. P., had this advice: "Listen to your heart. Believe in your dream. Examine where you find joy. What gives you joy? That's probably the clearest route to your soul's work."

Use your imagination
Our imagination is a powerful ally. First imagine what you would like to be. Then take steps to achieve it. Keep imagining the fulfillment of your desire, knowing your subconscious is at work to achieve it. Your subconscious mind is overflowing with ideas. Your true source of wealth emanates from your ideas. Find the one you love best so you can make a living at it. Imprint a picture of your desire in your mind. It will help with manifestation.

What's your perspective?
I read about a newly discovered tribe who lived deep in the jungle and encountered modern civilization for the first time. They had no knowledge of photographs and, when shown pictures of themselves, were unable to see anything on the prints they were given. We are in the process of developing ourselves and making the invisible both visible and comprehensible.

This book is designed to help change your perspective. It was only after artist Toni Onley taught sailors of Canada's Arctic Ocean about perspective that they were able to see the subtle shades of pink, blue, and mauve that he could see. Prior to that, all they saw was a sea of white.

Express your Creativity
Both art and science have created great works that evolved out of a dream, vision, or inspiration. When our creativity surfaces in our conscious awareness, it allows us to both play and work with it. In reality, each of us is always in the process of creating our own life through our choices.

The creative arts have always interested Boomers. Even those who couldn't draw made a tie-dyed shirt, dressed up their jeans with funky patches, or strummed on a guitar. Some chose a full-time career in the arts. Others are returning to the arts now that they have more free time. Aside from the fun factor, a bonus to the arts is that creative people tend to live longer. The better your imagination functions, the more options you can generate and the more choices you will have. Art also provides a vehicle with which to leave a piece of yourself behind.

Psychologists have been exploring ways to expand our creativity. Scientific American Mind (July/August 2012) gave a number of tips on how to put creativity to work. These included stepping out of your comfort zone and trying new experiences such as travelling to a foreign country or learning a new skill. They also suggested talking to outsiders about your work to get a new perspective—that may lead to alternate solutions; putting on some upbeat music; taking time to daydream a little; challenging yourself to improve on someone else's ideas; and visualizing yourself in the distant future, as opposed to the next day. Above all, they stress the willingness to take a risk. Your own creativity can help generate options—then choose the best one, and devise a plan to realize your vision.

Being illogical actually makes sense
Looking for the safe route will not create radical new solutions. We all know that we cannot create something new by doing the same thing over and over. Being innovative, though, disrupts the beaten path. Those who accomplish great things tend to think in a way that others see as illogical. Thomas Edison was illogical, as were the Wright brothers. Would a logical thinker have created a light bulb or thought he could fly like a bird?

It was Buckminster Fuller who advised that the way to change something is to build a new model that makes the old one obsolete. This thinking has led to the creation of new "green products." Remember to maintain your focus on what you want—not on what you don't want. You need to be able to fantasize about what you want before you can get it. Have a look at the notebooks of Leonardo da Vinci. They are filled with his fanciful ideas. "When the spirit does not work with the hand, there is no art," he claimed.

The best way to be positive about the future is to first be aware of what you don't like in the present. Then, follow the lead of Gandhi, work for what you want—rather than against something. Be for clean air rather than against pollution. Visualize what you do want your "ideal future" to look like. To work on your own terms, you must define those terms and believe you can achieve them.

Use visualization, in the same way Olympic athletes do. See yourself achieving the goals you have set for yourself. Create a vision board of your desires. We think in pictures. That's why we say a picture is worth a thousand words. Create a visual image of what you want. Post it where you can see it daily. It will keep you focused.

Brain scans have shown that our brain can't distinguish imagination from reality. The same areas light up on a scan when we imagine ourselves performing an activity, as when we are actually doing the activity. Create your ideal lifestyle in your imagination first, then rewire your brain to achieve it.

Creativity produces energy. Innovation can start our adrenaline pumping. When an artist creates, she is often stepping out of her comfort zone. Take a risk. Colour outside of the lines regardless of what you were taught in kindergarten. When you have fire in your belly (passion), you can do the impossible. Don't be afraid of mistakes. You'll make them. You can learn from them. Sometimes they'll lead you somewhere better than where you thought you were going.

"My job was killing my passion," said H. M., one of my interviewees, "When my passion left, the job was just a paycheque. I'm a thousand times more passionate now! There's no question. If there's one thing that's changed (since becoming self-employed), it's my passion for living."

In North America, we are free to embrace our creativity. Please use it. In many countries with military regimes, artists simply "disappear." Artists are often the link between progressive culture, politics, and social change.

The most valuable resource we bring to our work is our creativity. Everyone is creative. Not everyone owns this. Creative thinkers value ideas—both their own and those of others. They like to explore their options and look for some that veer away from the beaten path. Unusual ideas intrigue rather than scare them. They are willing to take a risk and don't fear failure. When Edison invented the light bulb after numerous unsuccessful attempts, he was asked about his failures. He said "I have not failed. I've just found ten thousand ways that won't work." Creativity and failure precede innovation.

When people think of creativity, they often envision artists and musicians. If they don't have natural talent in the arts, they believe they are not creative. Author Ernie Zelinski believes our creativity gets a boost when we don't automatically know all the answers. He suggests we tap into the unknown to use our creativity as a launching pad to generate possible solutions. He suggests "creativity is having options" (Zelinski, 1994).

Ideas are the seeds from which grow inventive ways to earn a living without a job. And ideas stem from creativity. We need to give ourselves permission to develop our creative side.

Many people discover their ideal work by fulfilling a need they themselves have experienced. For example, not having time to cook, clean, walk the dog, or run errands can lead to starting a business offering these services.

If you work somewhere that discourages creativity, you are likely to stop sharing your ideas after they get a cold reception. Nothing will shut down a brainstorming session faster than being interrupted with comments like "That won't work," "That's stupid," "We've already tried something similar," and so on. Find a workplace that allows creativity to flourish. It is a requirement for a successful business.

How to develop your creativity
To enhance your creativity, try something you've never done before. Intense concentration and focus are necessary to help the brain rewire. To keep your brain fit, you must learn something new, rather than reusing already mastered skills. Read new subjects. Study a new language. Learn how to play a musical instrument. Choose something you've always wanted to do. Travel somewhere you've never been. Explore other cultures and traditions. Get out of the all-expenses-included resort and mingle with the locals. Consider walking Spain's Camino de Santiago Pilgrim trail. A healthy pace will get your blood circulating and strengthen both your heart and the blood vessels that supply your brain while stimulating the growth of new neurons. It will also give you time to come up with some new ideas.

Dancer and choreographer Twyla Tharp shares her inspiration for creativity in her book, *The Creative Habit,* in a way that can help the rest of us. Creativity begins with preparation, ritual practice, and being open to it. She suggests replacing doubt and fear with comfort and routine, as a writer who might take a hot mug of coffee outside each morning in preparation to write and carries pen and paper to record inspiration as it arises.

Tharp choreographs each new dance in a white room devoid of clutter—so there is nothing to distract her from the creative process. You may need to eliminate your own distractions so you can focus. She cites some common fears that can arise when starting a creative project. She said people fear being laughed at, that they have nothing original to say, they might upset someone else with their work, or their idea may fall short of their own expectations. Her response to all of these is, "So what? Do it anyway."

The future of work
Innovation will be the key driver of economic advantage in the future. To get an idea of the unlimited opportunity available to us to create change for the better, check out the *Institute for Global Futures.*

James Canton, author of *The Extreme Future*, tells us we will need to be able to deal with complex change that will come even faster than before. He says customers are driving change, and the global demand for products and services is about to explode. Business owners will need to listen to customer needs, wants, and concerns and develop a systems approach to understanding the future—because everything is connected. He wants us to have a hand in shaping the future ourselves by collaborating with others. The essence of servant leadership is leading people in the direction they want to go.

Canton predicts innovation, collaboration, and a positive vision of the future will transform the future for the better. In fact, he says, they already have. He cites examples in nanoengineering, biotechnology, neuroscience, and quantum mechanics. Business must build protection of the environment into their products and services because customers are demanding it. People and businesses that are more reactive than proactive will lose out in the future. Ride the trends in the direction they are going.

Action Steps – Questions to Ponder

Let your imagination run wild.
What does your ideal life look like—in your wildest dreams?
Flip through magazines for inspiration.

Twyla Tharp uses a white room for her work. I see this as a metaphor for an uncluttered mind. Can you create a metaphor to describe your own work?

Can you create a visual representation of the work you want to do?

I walk clients through the steps of creating a "Soul Collage Card" as inspiration for their own work. I created a card with the image of a Boomer emerging from a blossoming flower—based on a quote from Anais Nin that I had clipped from a magazine (I have also used this quote at the beginning of my book): "And the day came when the risk to remain tight in a bud was more painful that the risk it took to blossom."

I cut from magazines the words "bloom," "dreams are in full bloom," "passion," "leaving a legacy," and another quote, this one from Annie Dillard, "Now is the season for all sorts of blossoming," along with pictures of flowers. Once my soul collage card was complete, it led me to calling my business, Blooming Boomers.

As most of us are visual, I suggest you create and then post your own card in your work area as a way to maintain your focus.

Soundtrack

Here's a song I wouldn't want sung at my funeral. Talk about lack of creativity in living. It's the message of the song:

Little boxes on the hillside.
Little boxes made of ticky tacky...
And they all look just the same.

"Little Boxes"
Malvina Reynolds

Is this really how you want to live your life?

Books You Might Like to Read

The Artist's Way
by Julia Cameron

The War of Art
by Steven Pressfield

Artful Work
by Dick Richards

The Creative Habit
by Twyla Tharp

Also Google

John Cleese on Creativity (YouTube video)

Chapter 22:
Awaken Your Intuition

Intuition is another form of perception. We simply need to tap into it more often. I'm sure you've received a message from your intuition. Did you pay attention to it? The most dramatic message I have received was while out driving. I had an inner voice telling me to get off the road as there was about to be an accident. No sooner had I pulled over to the shoulder than a five-car pileup happened right beside me. I pay more attention to my intuition now.

Our intuition can help us access more of our potential. It can provide insight and guidance beyond our rational thought process. It is connected with our heart. It bypasses our intellect. We often believe it is hard work that will get us where we want to go. If you have felt like a salmon swimming upstream most of your life, you will welcome getting in touch with your intuition. It has the power to take you down the path of least resistance. Trust the guidance you receive.

We are not surprised when we hear that artists follow their intuition. We may be surprised to hear that nearly all scientific discoveries also arose from creative flashes of intuitive insight. You can tap into your unconscious mind in the same way as Dr. Frederick Banting, Edison, Marconi, and Einstein did prior to sharing their discoveries with the world.

Trusting intuition requires tuning out the external world and listening for internal cues. A common method of doing this is to simply think about a question that needs answering and then dream on it, allowing your subconscious to provide the answer upon awakening. It is helpful to have pen and paper close by to record any insights that come to you. Trust them to be what is best for you.

R. B., another one of the people I interviewed for my Master's thesis, explained how intuition guides her work: "Now, I'm very choosy about the kind of work I do. It really has to fit in with my values. I'm very intuitive, and I choose things that feel right."

Quiet your mind so you can listen
Listening to the beat of a drum can cause the brain to slow down into a trancelike state. Shamanic cultures practice this method to activate the soul's knowledge. Research has demonstrated that drumming produces changes in the central nervous system. Rhythmic drumming can induce an altered state of consciousness, opening us to receive information in the form of intuition.

Quieting the mind is vital to consciously access intuition. Meditation is an excellent tool you can use to cultivate your inner knowing. We are often so bombarded by noise that it becomes difficult to hear our own voice. It's distracting when your cellphone is ringing, the TV is blaring, music is playing, and there is a leaf blower outside your window. Find a way to block out the noise.

Stop *doing* for a while and just *be*. Sit quietly for fifteen minutes each day—and just listen. As Lao Tzu said, "Nothing is more powerful and creative than emptiness."

A focused mind will serve and guide you. The more you choose to focus your attention, the more information is revealed. Still your mind and body, be in the present moment, pose a question and then be receptive to the answer. An answer will come. Be aware that your logical mind will often question it.

Universal mind refers to our collective consciousness. Every one of us can tap into this at any time *(the one hundredth monkey syndrome)*. Pay attention to your gut feelings. They will indicate when you are on the wrong path. If you deny your intuition, your body may send you red flags in the form of depression, anxiety, or mood swings. Listen for the message behind those feelings. Take time to reflect, review, and revise.

Following your intuition will put you in the flow of the forces of life. Focus on what you truly want. The real power of intuition is that it gives you the power to change your destiny and create a new reality— should you choose to follow it. Intuition is part of the magic of life. Be open to it.

Any form of dis-ease in our lives can signal an imbalance. It can slow us down long enough to re-evaluate where we are and where we are going. Illness might be nature's way of prodding us to make changes. Intuition enables us to hear things we may not want to hear. It can tell us how we feel about something, why we feel that way, and what to do about it.

If you are struggling to access who you are at the core and what your gifts are, I suggest you have a look at the following tools for guidance. You will soon know if the explanations resonate with you, or not.

Myers-Briggs Type Indicator ™
The Myers-Briggs Type Indicator (MBTI) assumes we are born with our gifts. In midlife, we have more time to utilize those gifts— sometimes for the first time. I recommend you find someone qualified to administer and interpret the MBTI for you. In the meantime, I'll give you a very brief introduction to get you started.

Each person has a set of specific gifts to work with. This is what forms our personality temperament. This is one tool career counsellors often use to help clients gain insight into their character and preferences. No MBTI types are exactly alike, even though at first glance it looks as if there are only sixteen of them. We are as different as snowflakes. What makes you uniquely you?

When your work engages the core of who you are, your stress level will decrease. Conversely, if you feel completely stressed at work, it is likely not the best fit for you. The MBTI suggests types of work that might resonate with you. My favourite book on this topic is *Do What You Are.*

Without knowing your MBTI type, you can still answer the following:

What percentage of your time would you like to work with others, versus the percentage of time you would like to work alone?

What percentage of your time would you like to spend concentrating on practical facts, figures, or other details, versus the amount of time you would like to devote to innovation or creativity?

What percentage of your time would you like to spend using your logical, objective thinking, versus using your person-centred values and emotions?

What percentage of time would you like to be able to work in an orderly, organized manner, versus being able to be spontaneous and open to new opportunities?

Look for work that will provide the right mix for you. For example, if you enjoy interacting with people most of the time, you will likely not enjoy working on your own in a back office all day. If you enjoy solo work as much as you enjoy working as part of a team, you might want work that will offer more of a fifty-fifty mix.

Multiple Intelligences you might possess
You are likely familiar with IQ tests that were administered when you attended school. Howard Gardner has identified nine intelligences that IQ tests may have missed. You may want to visit his work to help identify your inborn talent and to generate some career ideas for yourself. Here are the nine intelligences he will guide you through: an ability to connect deeply with the natural world (naturalist); musical talent; logical/mathematical reasoning; an

understanding of the deeper meaning of life (existential); interpersonal skills with others; knowledge about how to use your body for dance or athletics (bodily-kinesthetic); an ability with words (verbal-linguistic); strong self-knowledge (intra-personal); and an aptitude for thinking in 3-D pictures (visual-spatial). People have successful careers using each of these intelligences.

Gardner has written a number of books on this topic, including *Intelligence Reframed: Multiple Intelligences for the 21st Century.* If you Google his name, you will find a lot more information online.

Do you prefer to work with

people, animals, plants, information, ideas, or tools?

What special talents do you have?

Which skills do you most enjoy using?

What is your preferred environment to live and work in:
(Inside or outside? Big company, small company, at home? Formal or informal atmosphere?)

Education—Do you need additional training? Can you get it for free through volunteer work? Can you pay for it yourself? Don't be afraid to invest in your own future.

Which topics are of most interest to you?
(Visit your local public library to explore the books and magazines that most interest you.)

Action Steps – Questions to Ponder

What is your heart telling you to do?

Have you ever felt you knew what your dream career was, but your logical brain said you'd never make a living at it?
(Does your logical brain know about the guy who made millions selling pet rocks and splintered pieces of the Brooklyn Bridge?)

Books You Might Like to Read

Do What Your Are (about the MBTI)
by Tieger, Paul D., and Barbara Barron-Tieger

This book has helped guide many people toward their chosen career path. It can be especially helpful if you feel confused about which line of work would fulfill you. You may discover you have already worked at what you love in the past—but have accidentally veered off in a different direction.

I See Your Dream Job
by Sue Frederick

This book may seem a bit more "out there," as it is based on numerology. It defines your destiny based on how your birthdates add up. Although it seems like fortune-telling, the answer was accurate for me. Have a look at it.

Also Google

Myers-Briggs Type Indicator
Kiersey Temperament Sorter
Multiple Intelligences—Howard Gardner

Chapter 23:
Set Your Intention

The artist is the servant of intention.

Steven Pressfield

Your highest future possibility is related to your own highest purpose or intention. It's more an intention you build for yourself, for your life, perhaps even before you are born.

Peter Senge

Intention is what gives us the power to manifest our desires. It is connected to our purpose. Intention has infinite organizing power. It is how we ask for assistance from our Higher Power. Once you have a crystal clear intention of what you want to experience in life, you can move mountains. When you create a concrete statement of how you would like to live, it seems as if all the forces of the universe somehow align to make it happen.

Without clear intention, we lack direction. I'm sure you've heard the saying, "If you don't know where you're going, any road will take you there." The problem is—will you like where "there" is once you arrive? If you are not able to envision a better life for yourself, your current reality is likely your future.

This book invites you to set the intention to work on your own terms and to then take steps to determine how you will do it. After you have made this commitment, synchronicity will start sending you pieces of the puzzle that will fit the life you dream of. You will start to meet people who are already working on their own terms, come across a book on the topic, or perhaps it will be the theme of a movie you watch.

It was by setting a clear intention that a friend of mine completely transformed her life. She was an unemployed social worker who at age fifty decided she wanted to become a mediator. She set a clear intention to become one—and now not only is she a mediator, but she managed to be paid while training and has tripled her income in the process. This is the real power of intention. I believe we are never too old to make our dreams come true.

When you are able to set a clear intention and then act on it to demonstrate your commitment, I am confident amazing things will occur for you as well. Staying totally focused on your end goal will also help you weather any problems along the way.

You might want to start with small goals. Set an intention to have fun tomorrow no matter what. Or set an intention to find a parking spot downtown or to stay calm during an interview and see what happens.

Intention works on an invisible wavelength. Imagine wanting to listen to your favourite radio channel—let's say The Ocean at 98.7 on the FM dial. You will tune in with the intention of receiving that station. If there is interference, you will keep fine-tuning until the static has cleared and you are receiving a clear channel. Once you know what you want to receive, you don't keep changing the channel; you tune into that frequency and stay there.

You will stop "fiddling with the dial"—changing your mind about what you want to receive—or the airwaves will be nothing but jumbled static. That's the simple secret of the power of intention. Decide what you want, then tune in to receive it, knowing with certainty that you will. You don't "hope" the radio station is still there; you don't "wish" it would pop into your radio—you know it's there; you just need to tune into it. There are many scientific research studies that prove this. If you would like more scientific evidence read *The Field: The Quest for the Secret Force of the Universe,* by Lynne McTaggart.

We are all creating our own works of art with our lives. Are you clear about what you really want? What is your intent? Until you figure that out, you are like a starving beggar at the "banquet of life" who dillies and dallies so long that others eat all the food or it rots on the table. Decide what you want so you can focus on it. Maintain your focus on what you want rather than on what you don't want. Worrying about a high unemployment rate will not help you find work.

Edward Mills speaks of the power of intention. He was part of the 2012 Project. He helped create the Birth 2012 Movement to celebrate the birth of a New Era that began on December 21. It was a global thirty-three-hour webcast organized by The Shift Network to unify people globally around a commitment to create a world that works for all. It included bestselling authors, musicians, and cultural leaders. The intention was to continue to build a critical mass of people committed to positive change.

Mills warns us not to become paralyzed by information overload. Get to the core of who you are and what you want. He says people who are both spiritually and monetarily rich know they can create whatever they desire. They choose what they want rather than focusing on what they don't want. They are 100 percent confident they will get what they want. They don't hesitate to act on their ideas. They get out of their comfort zone and trust their intuition. They act on their intentions without forcing things to happen, while maintaining an attitude of gratitude.

Express who you are at your core. This first requires self-knowledge. The reason a butterfly emerges from a cocoon rather than a grasshopper is because the caterpillar becomes what it is. It doesn't sit around in its cocoon wondering what it should be when it grows up. It becomes its purpose. Who you are is in you as well. You just need to release it. Unlike the caterpillar, we have the power to continue to grow and reinvent ourselves. I think of it more as finding our way back home.

Becoming more conscious of our choices will enable us to change how we think about ourselves and how we relate to the world around us. We are capable of affecting our larger world through our intention and where we place our attention.

Peter Senge believes the difference between the science practiced by First Nations communities and Western science begins with intent. While Western science strives to understand nature so we can control it, native science strives to let us live in harmony with nature.

Senge asks us to examine our own intention for how we wish to create the world we live in. His beliefs are similar to those of Edgar Cayce, who believed the seeds of possibility for our lives were planted in us through some mysterious process prior to our birth. Our life's work is to uncover and work with what we were born to do. The evidence is contained in our inborn gifts. Native American teacher Phil Lane teaches that "the longest road you will ever walk is the sacred journey from your head to your heart."

Where you put your attention is what you will create. Don't put your attention on things that weaken you or that you don't want.

When I look back, I can see the power of intention in my own life, although I didn't call it that at the time. I was focused on what I wanted. I travelled twice for extended periods of time in my twenties. Even though I was not earning much more than minimum wage, I focused on my goal of travelling which caused me to dramatically reduce expenses and increase my savings.

When I decided to move to the West Coast, I set my moving date a year in advance and relocated exactly a year later. Setting the date caused me to work backwards on the action steps I needed to complete. Stephen Covey, educator, author, and businessman, termed this "beginning with the end in mind."

When I envisioned my perfect apartment, I wrote out everything I was looking for—and moved in less than a week later, in spite of an extremely competitive rental market. It was on the top floor, had a south-facing balcony, a view of the Olympic Mountains, and a working fireplace. I didn't even know apartments came with fireplaces when I placed this on my wish list—especially in the exact neighbourhood I wanted.

So, intention really works! In spite of this, it took me more than fifteen years to translate this into designing a way to work on my own terms. Fear can trump intention every time. Don't let it beat you.

The older we get, the more we need to stay focused on our goals if we want to have any hope of achieving them. Our most important decisions will be the ones that relate to the purpose we have set for our lives. Remain focused on the life you want to live. Keep reminding yourself why you want this lifestyle. It is by following through on our intentions and accepting the associated costs that we create a life worth living.

Focus your intention
It is essential for you to find your own voice so you can express who you really are both in life and work. No two people are alike. That is why a one-size-fits-all job description is insufficient.

Hypnosis proves the brain is susceptible to the power of directed thought. The placebo effect has shown the mind to be a more powerful healer than drugs. We are constantly remaking our world through our thoughts—whether they are positive or negative, conscious or unconscious.

The Law of Attraction tells us that we can only attain what we desire when we are able to consistently get in touch with how we will feel once we have it. How do you expect to feel when you are working on your own terms? Maintain that feeling while working towards your goal. What I feel about my work is true joy in having the freedom to use my skills to make a difference in the lives of others. As Maslow termed it, I feel self-actualized. My intention with this book is that it will lead you to experience something similar.

What about the money?
Financial well-being can be a form of proof we are living "on purpose." I say this because I believe in the adage "do what you love, and the money will follow." If you need to make an income, why would you not want to do something you enjoy? If you work at something you dislike, no amount of money will compensate.

Interviewee J. T. explained her transition from employee to self-employment this way: "My quality of life is much greater than the financial reward— but I need less now. It's so ideal what I do. I'm making a life, but not necessarily a living—but for me, I'm making enough, and that's plenty. My quality of life is now far superior to what I had. I need less now." Another solopreneur, D. S. said, "I never plan to retire. I have no desire to because I get paid to do what I enjoy."

It is pointless to spend time being anxious or worried about how you will be able to work on your own terms. Decide what you want; then take steps to attain it. Stay focused. If you are walking down a path towards the beach and a pebble gets in your shoe, you shake it out and carry on. Do the same with your fears as you walk toward your goals. Our true power comes from alignment with our intention. The only obstacle is our resistance.

Mihaly Csikszentmihalyi, a college professor, has written about the importance of working with "flow." He emphasized that "the best moments of life are those when our minds and bodies are stretched to the limit in a voluntary effort to accomplish something we find worthwhile."

Know that once your intention is clear, it will manifest. Focus on who you want to be and the path for how to do it will open up.

Action Steps

Take your dreams seriously. By setting an intention, you will make it clear to yourself and others what you plan to do.

8 Steps to Manifest Your Intention:

1. Become consciously aware of what you want.
2. Write it down so you can read it daily.
3. Take small action steps every week.
4. Recognize any fears that arise and move through them.
5. Choose to release your resistance to change.
6. Share your intention with someone who can support you and keep you accountable for your actions.
7. Keep focused and moving forward.
8. Recognize the manifestation of your desires.

After becoming the first person to stand on the continental divide, explorer Lewis Meriwether, on the eve of his thirty-first birthday, exclaimed: "Ask yourself: Have I done enough for the happiness of mankind? Have I done enough to further the knowledge of future generations?"

Soundtrack 🎵

"We May Never Pass This Way Again"
Seals and Crofts

Life, so they say
is but a game and we let it slip away.

Books You Might Like to Read

Browse the biography section of your local library and read a biography that inspires you.

The Field: The Quest for the Secret Force of the Universe by Lynne McTaggart.

The Power of Intention by Wayne Dyer

Awakening Intention by Mona Lisa Schulz

V.
FEAR OF OLD AGE

Chapter 24:
Use Your Time Wisely

Millions long for immortality who do not know what to do with themselves on a rainy Sunday afternoon.

Susan Ertz

It's hard to teach a young dog old tricks.

Warren Buffet

In Warren Buffet's words, "Sixty-five is just getting started—age and experience can be far greater virtues than youth and enthusiasm."

The best antidotes to the fear of old age are likely moderate exercise, restful sleep, healthy food, a positive attitude, close friends and family, prayer or meditation, and doing what you love.

Napoleon Hill believed this fear stems from two sources: the fear that with old age comes poverty, and the fear of what awaits us in the afterlife. The possibility of ill health in old age also contributes to this fear. It is primarily the loss of freedom and independence that many fear—a loss of both physical and economic freedom.

If you are able to live fully in the present moment, fear of old age and death will dissolve, since the only time that exists is now. The only way to live in the past or future is in your mind, and we have already discussed how to harness control over a wandering mind. Time is always available for us to use as we wish; problems arise when we waste it. Common phrases about time have entered our vernacular. How often have we heard comments like "I don't have enough time," or "I'm just killing time"? We each have the same twenty-four hours a day, but we don't all choose to use time wisely.

If, for example, you are going to spend your day worrying, complaining, watching junk TV programs, or binge eating—at least do it consciously. If people feel pressed for time, they're probably spending too much time on activities that are meaningless to them. When you are working with flow—you are never short of time. In fact, you lose track of time as you are one with the present moment. To bring yourself back to the present moment, ask yourself if the activity you are performing serves your core values. It is when we dishonour our values that we feel burned out and frustrated about time.

Many traditions, including Native Americans' and Buddhists', recognize midlife as the time to take on one's life work. Our job is to find out who we are and to live "on purpose." There is no need to apologize for your age. Hopefully the years have brought wisdom along with laugh lines and grey hair.

Consider this: sometimes, the more mould there is on a cheese, the more we appreciate it. Rather than trying to prolong our youth, what would happen if we began to appreciate the aging process in a similar fashion to the way we appreciate a fine wine that goes along with the cheese?

As Eckhart Tolle suggests in *A New Earth*, "As your awareness increases and the ego is no longer running your life, you don't have to wait for your world to shrink or collapse through old age or personal tragedy in order for you to awaken to your inner purpose."

Action Steps

Go for a walk in nature. Fully absorb and engross yourself in your surroundings, using all your senses.

Spend at least fifteen minutes a day just being
—not doing anything.

Savour it.

Soundtrack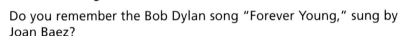

Do you remember the Bob Dylan song "Forever Young," sung by Joan Baez?

May God's blessings keep you always,
May your wishes all come true,
May you always do for others,
And let others do for you . . .
And may you stay forever young.

I think Boomers will be forever young in spirit.

Chapter 25:
Live In The Present Moment

I am myself at this age. It took me all these years to put the missing pieces together, to confront my own age in terms of integrity and generativity, moving into the unknown future with comfort now, instead of being stuck in the past. I have never felt so free.

Betty Friedan

Live in each season as it passes;
breathe the air, drink the drink, taste the fruit.

Henry David Thoreau

Although many of us appear to believe otherwise, the only time we have is now. Practice the art of living in the present moment.

The Story of 1,000 Marbles
Here's a story I read online a few years ago, written by Jeffrey Davis. See what you think of it.

Davis said he was listening in on his ham radio when he heard an older man speaking with a younger man who said he was working 60 to 70 hours a week, causing him to miss important family events.

The older man said he would like to tell him how he had prioritized his own life. He said one day he realized the average lifespan is about 75 years. When he multiplied 75 by the number of weeks in a year, he calculated that added up to about 3,900 Saturdays in an average lifetime. When the older man reached age 55, that thought came back to him, and he realized he had about 1000 Saturdays left, if he was to live to age 75.

He decided to create a visual reminder for himself by buying 1000 marbles. He placed them in a bowl and every Saturday, he removed one of the marbles to remind himself of the passage of time. He was speaking to the younger man on the day he had removed his last marble. He then said goodbye to the younger man as he had a breakfast date with his wife (Davis, 1999).

Can you create a visual reminder to keep yourself focused on your dreams?

Keep a Gratitude Journal

Gratitude is the first sign of a thinking, rational creature.
And it is also what enables us to be fully human.

Solanus Casey

One of the world's leading experts on the power of gratitude is Robert A, Emmons, PhD. Through his research, he has discovered that gratitude plays a critical role in human happiness. His work found that a regular practice of feeling gratitude *(such as keeping a daily gratitude journal)* has helped people improve their lives on a physical, psychological, and social level.

Emmons concluded that "gratitude is one of the few attitudes that can measurably change people's lives." This is because it helps us focus on what is right in our world rather than on what is *wrong* with it. Gratitude helps anchor us in the present. It stops us from taking things for granted (Emmons, 2013). Consider counting your blessings every day in a journal and remember the words of Ram Das to "be here now."

Action Steps – Questions to Ponder

Calculate how many Saturdays you think you have left.
There is no such thing as "not enough time."
You decide what your priorities are.

Frequently ask yourself: Is this the best use of my time?
Act only on your top priorities.

What are you grateful for?
Consider keeping a gratitude journal.

Soundtrack:

"The Dutchman"
Steve Goodman

Long ago I used to be a young man.
And dear Margaret remembers that for me.

Books You Might Like to Read

Tuesdays With Morrie
by Mitch Albom

The Power of Now
by Eckhart Tolle

Be Here Now
by Ram Das

Chapter 26:
A Life Of Purpose

There comes a time when you ought to start doing what you want. Take a job that you love. You will jump out of bed in the morning. I think you are out of your mind if you keep taking jobs you don't like because you think they will look good on your resumé . . . Do what you love and the money will come.

Warren Buffett

This is true joy—
being used for a purpose recognized by yourself as a mighty one.

George Bernard Shaw

At some level, we all hunger for our lives to have meaning. Our purpose comes from using our skills to help others. Think about Terry Fox, Gandhi, Mother Theresa, or former President Jimmy Carter. What are you doing with your life? What is your life's work? What legacy will you leave behind?

Most people have not taken the time to discover their purpose. They've just been trying to make it through to Friday or retirement. Make time—even if only for fifteen minutes a day. Take the time to stop, be quiet, and just contemplate.

Your purpose is greater than your goals. It's your big picture. It represents your ideal dream. To live life to the fullest, your goals need to reflect your purpose. Craig Kielburger was only twelve when he decided his life mission would be to "free the children" from child labour.

My ideal dream is to have Boomers live happily working on their own terms, while making a difference in the lives of others. What do you care deeply enough about that you could dedicate the rest of your life to? Anything that sparks your interest is a clue you can follow to see where it leads. Don't settle for a life of mediocrity.

Robert Byrne said, "The purpose of life is a life of purpose." Your purpose stems from something you have a natural gift for. What are your special skills and talents? What do you really enjoy doing? I tend to be good at generating ideas and speaking up as a catalyst for change. *(The MBTI is a tool that can help uncover your gifts.)*

If you have a strong interest in a subject, you likely have talent in that field. Both learning and creativity can cure boredom. Involvement in a project you have passion for can be healing. I hope you have already begun a conscious search for the underlying theme that pulls your interests together. My theme is self-knowledge and helping others to trust their instinct and get to know themselves better. We can all find our place and our meaning in the world.

How can you make a difference? First, answer why you want to achieve your goals. What is it you have a burning desire to do? Who will you help in the process? Don't be distracted by the naysayers. Always focus on what you can do—not on what you can't. Delegate what others can do better.

Don't seek out fame and fortune or Hollywood-style trappings. Just do your work. The rewards will follow. They may be much deeper than you expected. Think about how the lives of Nelson Mandela and Mother Theresa unfolded while they remained on their chosen path.

Most of us make our choices automatically, unconsciously, without even realizing we are making a choice. This will lead to an "accidental future." Are you waiting for *good luck* to define your future? I happily throw a dollar a week into a group lottery pool—but I'm not just sitting around waiting for my lucky numbers to be called. It's just a game I play. I don't decide the rules. My life is too precious not to design my own game plan.

There is a man in the downtown streets where I often walk who has created his own purpose. I read about him in our local newspaper. He is a homeless man who has been unable to find a job. I think he may have some form of mental disability. He decided to create his own work out of a need he saw. He built a cart out of discarded parts he found and every day he walks the streets picking up trash. The streets are cleaner because of this man. He moves swiftly, and with purpose. He does not ask for handouts. Occasionally, I am able to catch up with him to thank him for his work and to give him a donation, for which he is always grateful. The street cleaner has made his purpose visible. We are not all here for something dramatic like finding the cure for cancer. What purpose can you create for yourself? Decide what you do best and then just do it.

By making conscious choices, we can override old programming that created old habits. We can begin to create new, more positive and productive self-programming of our subconscious mind so we can live with purpose and meaning. People with unclear goals, a fuzzy picture of themselves, who make unclear choices, end up with an unclear future. Once your choices are clear, you will give more energy to making those choices work.

Carl Jung noted his belief that "nothing is a stronger influence psychologically on people than the unlived lives of their parents." Over time, suppressing one's individuality will take a toll on one's health— emotionally, physically, or both. It is ultimately up to us to define our own sense of purpose and then to live it.

Allow yourself to be who you were meant to be. An animal doesn't wonder what it should be when it grows up. It is what it is. Sometimes our big brain gets in the way of our being who we are. Figure out who you are at your core and then be it.

Your life purpose is not always what you do to earn a living. It can be more a theme that weaves through your life story. It could be a challenge that keeps reappearing throughout your life. We may not view this as a "gift that keeps on giving," but it may hold the key to your treasure—the Holy Grail of your life purpose.

Action Steps – Questions to Ponder

What is the greatest challenge in your life that keeps repeating itself?

Is there a lesson in that challenge that you can teach others?

Is there anything that tugs at your heartstrings, and you can't ignore it?

In one, simple sentence, what's your purpose?
Your purpose may begin as a dream. Turn it into a goal by setting both a start date and a finish date for when you will launch it into reality.

Here's my Personal Statement of Purpose

My purpose is to help Boomers realize they can live and work on their own terms in midlife and beyond.

Please note: Your purpose and mission statement should overlap. They are often exactly the same.

If you have watched the Knowledge Network TV program, Hope For Wildlife, you will be familiar with the tagline, "Hope for Wildlife . . . because they matter." The official mission statement of the wildlife sanctuary is: "Connecting people to wildlife in a positive way—through knowledge and understanding—the Hope for Wildlife Society believes that education through rehabilitation is the key to a sustainable future."

You might want to use this as an example to write your own.

Soundtrack ♪

"100 Years to Live"
Five for Fighting

Another blink of an eye, 67 is gone
The sun is getting high. We're moving on.

No book or Internet suggestions this time

Just a recommendation that you write the story of your own life. It doesn't need to take the form of a book.

Chapter 27:
Show Some Emotion

I did not lose myself all at once. I rubbed out my face over the years washing away my pain, the same way carvings on stone are worn down by water.

Amy Tan

Whenever you experience strong emotions, it is your soul's way of communicating with you. What are your emotions trying to tell you? This is what an artist taps into to inspire her work. Negative emotions can be a clue that something in your life needs healing. Listen to your intuition to decode your emotions.

Use midlife as a time to heal any "unfinished business." If you have been laid off, acknowledge any feelings of anger, hurt, fear, betrayal, panic, or even relief and joy. What message do these emotions convey to you?

Rather than trying to become a better person through self-improvement courses, consider undoing the steps where you lost yourself. When Michelangelo created his statue of David, he said he chipped away at everything that wasn't him in order to release his essence. Release yourself from your own marble casing. Even if you are trapped in marble, gold, furs, mountains of shoes, or a mansion with a moat, you are still trapped. Ask yourself what choices and decisions you made to get there. Be willing to experience more of yourself. Anything that really upsets you can be a gold mine to explore who you are.

Your body is like a photographic plate. It records your emotions. Emotions empower your thoughts. What you think and feel affects your body. Monitoring what you think and feel is the road to enlightenment. Practice being aware of yourself in the present moment. Don't repress your emotions, because eventually you will need to vent them. Our thoughts, feelings, and what we say all create the universe. Denial of responsibility is also a denial of our power. How we treat the earth reflects how we treat ourselves.

Our emotional guidance system will lead us toward our desire if we allow it. Tap into this guidance by first being aware of it. Emotional honesty is infectious. It is the foundation of genuine connection with others. It is critical in friendship and in a successful business.

Our emotions often create spontaneous reactions to situations triggered by memories and past conditioning. Virginia Satir, author and psychotherapist, dedicated her life to helping people realize how early childhood conditioning was embedded in them before they learned to speak. To successfully focus our emotional energy, we need to stay tuned into what our bodies are trying to communicate to us. It was Robert Frost who wrote "Before I built a wall, I'd ask what I was walling in or walling out."

In *The Authentic Career*, Maggie Craddock wrote "Our bodies are the gatekeepers of the feelings we allow ourselves to experience and the memories we allow ourselves to access." Scientists have researched the way we store memories, not just in our skulls, but in our every cell and atom. If we store memories in our bodies as well as our minds, then mental awareness only tackles the challenge of eliminating limiting beliefs from what we consciously think. We often assume, incorrectly, that what we think is more important than what we feel.

We need to get in touch with what our feelings and emotions are trying to tell us. If we were shut down in childhood, we are likely to act out those emotions as an adult. We can only truly heal once we are in touch with our emotions. Your conscious mind may have recorded a message that is more superficial than that recorded by your body. It registers everything in the subconscious, at the cellular level. Intuitive insights are connected with your emotions. What are they telling you? Pay attention to the signs and symptoms your body is sending your way.

We may need to dig deep to release any emotionally charged feelings and beliefs. To achieve meaningful change, we need to have all aspects of ourselves present. The path to achieving our authentic goals must meld our body, mind, and spirit. We need to shed our old skin before we can grow a new one. Resist the temptation to suppress negative emotions. They contain vast amounts of energy, and we know energy cannot be destroyed. Instead, bring them to the surface so you can examine them.

Become conscious of when you slip into a role that is not your authentic self. Office politics can bring out the worst in us, if we allow it to. Be true to yourself and don't give your power away. *(To see this in action and to second guess your own behaviour in a similar situation, just watch the Parliamentary Debates. Yikes! Talk about unresolved issues.)*

Growing up with an authoritarian father likely explains why I have had trouble respecting authoritarian leaders who bark out orders from above. Rather than react, this knowledge now allows me to look at those same leaders and wonder about their own childhoods.

Learning to hear the voice within and trusting our natural instinct will give us more freedom for creative expression. Our knowledge of brain plasticity can lead the way to enabling us to reprogram ourselves on our own conscious terms. Several people, including Oscar Wilde, have said "one's real life is often the life that one does not lead." Whenever we catch ourselves thinking a thought that does not serve our new life choices, we can choose a new thought. If previously you were fed thoughts of unworthiness, you can now choose to brush them off.

Recognize that other people and outer circumstances do not control us without our permission, and the approval of others doesn't count for much if we don't approve of our own behaviour. Others are not responsible for how we feel—we are. Become aware of how you feel. Golda Meir said, "Those who don't know how to weep with their whole heart don't know how to laugh either."

Our most deeply held values and beliefs represent our most emotionally charged thoughts. We have powerful feelings that have fueled these beliefs. Identify what the *shoulds* are in your life. How do they differ from your true desires? Whenever we say we should do something, someone else is directing our thoughts. Whenever we think or speak the word *should*, we are giving our power away. Reclaim your power.

Whenever we experience emotional pain, it's a signal that something matters to us. It is when we run away from pain that problems arise. It is our fear of emotional pain that often has us running in the opposite direction. Ironically, it is when we show our vulnerability that we reveal our greatest strength.

The heart has been called the "largest brain" in the body. Our emotions register deep in our intestines, hence the term *gut feelings*. An emotion like envy can be used in a positive way. If you notice what causes you to feel envy, it helps you identify what you want in life. Then you can figure out what you need to do to get the results you desire.

Our ability to face difficult emotions is essential to living a meaningful life. Whenever we choose to avoid our fears, they continue to control us. Putting a lid on our emotions only encourages the pot to boil over like a pressure cooker that eventually explodes on the ceiling. This may explain why sometimes people are surprised when their neighbour commits a horrendous crime when "he was such a nice boy."

Health professionals are starting to think suppressing difficult emotions may also cause disease to form as people turn their pain inward. It is our avoidance of pain that makes life difficult because it increases our suffering and prevents us from living the lives we want to lead.

Show Some Emotion

You may have heard the story of a woman who captured a cocoon so she could watch it transform into a moth. When she saw the moth struggling to free itself of its cocoon, she decided to help it out. The moth died soon after it emerged because it had needed the struggle to strengthen its wings. Pain and struggle are prerequisites to living our values. Is there a struggle that will help you strengthen your wings so you can fly? The easy way out doesn't usually lead to a values-based life.

Role models for Boomers are all around us
There are many inspiring role models for Boomers. Actor Betty White is more popular than ever. Many bands of our youth are still on tour. The Rolling Stones just keep on rocking and rolling. I feel blessed to have moved to a community with many active and engaged seniors. These are my role models. I sing alongside women in their eighties and nineties. I'm surrounded by talented artists of all ages—including many who are long past the typical "retirement" age. I'm sure if you look, you'll find similar role models in your own community.

I have numerous neighbours who prove the theory that creative types live longer, healthier, and happier lives. One of the oldest is a ninety-two-year-old Shakespearean actor, Antony Holland. After being forced to retire from teaching acting at a local college when he turned sixty-five, he created his own theatre group. Last year he wrote a play about his war years. He is currently on the road with it and receiving rave reviews. He once told me he would like to die on stage at the closing act of the play, *Tuesdays With Morrie.* He has played the role of Morrie to perfection a number of times.

Naomi Beth Wakan started writing professionally in her sixties. She gradually found her voice through writing, largely due to what she terms "the very practical problem of meeting a mortgage." She has currently written more than thirty books and delights her fellow Islanders with regular readings. Through both her workshops and her writing, she encourages budding Boomer authors. Now in her eighties, she has not only survived breast cancer but has thrived after writing about it.

Gary Fjellgaard, now aged seventy-five, is another Island treasure. He has been a wandering country minstrel for more than thirty years. Although Gary has won many awards and accolades for his Western Roots Music, he is best-loved at home for writing what has become our Island anthem. We sing it together every chance we get. It is aptly called "Islanders." I first heard this song while living in Toronto. It became a siren call beckoning me to the Gulf Islands.

Action Steps – Questions to Ponder

People who are fulfilling their potential have found their voice and are living their values. *Look around your neighbourhood. Find someone older than you who is working on his or her own terms. Ask them about it.*

How did they manage to work on their own terms?

Did they ever doubt themselves?

Is their work just a lucky accident or deliberate intention?

If you were told you only had five years left to live, what would you do?

What if it was only one year?

Six months?
Use this exercise to get yourself focused on what has meaning for you.

If you had enough money in the bank to be able to work at whatever you wanted—whether you were paid or not, what would you do?

How do your current activities contribute (or do not) to your sense of what is meaningful and important to you?

What could you do that would indicate that you were living on purpose?

I guess the reason songs have popped into my head throughout this book is that music often tugs at our emotions, creating what I've termed the Soundtrack.

Soundtrack

"Islanders"
Gary Fjellgaard

Islanders, Islanders, right to the bone,
How could we wander so far from our home?
With our true love beside us, we are kissed by the sea,
Islanders we'll always be.

Books You Might Like to Read

Late Bloomer
Ageing
A Gabriola Year
by Naomi Beth Wakan

My Private Parts (Biography of Antony Holland)
by James Hawkins

Also Google

Antony Holland
Naomi Beth Wakan
Gary Fjellgaard

When you stand and share your story in an empowering way,
your story will heal you and your story will heal someone else.

Iyanla Vanzant

VI.
FEAR OF DEATH

Chapter 28:
What's Your Mission?

The tragedy of life is not death, but what we let die inside us while we live.

Norman Cousins

At the end of our lifetime, it matters to us how well we pushed past our fears to live up to our mission . . . Harness the energy of fear to move you forward.

Sue Frederick

When Steve Jobs, co-founder of Apple Inc., became ill, he said, "Remembering that I'll be dead soon is the most important tool I've ever encountered to help me make the big choices in life." The irony is people who ponder their own mortality lead more fulfilling lives. People do not lie on their deathbed wishing they had spent more time at the mall. Those who exclaim: "Those shoes are to die for," are really just kidding.

Holistic health physician Deepak Chopra says it is death that makes life possible and that we really have no beginning or end. Dan Millman, author and lecturer, says, "Life itself is a near-death experience—ephemeral and brief . . . And every life represents a hero's journey, and every moment counts." Wayne Dyer, self-help author and motivational speaker, says, "The essential mission of your life is to go back to (or get to know) your originating source before physical death."

The average North American will live to age seventy-eight, with one-third of that time spent asleep. It is our choices, intentions, and actions that create the life we lead. You still have time to do what matters most to you. Take action to live your values. It is what you will be remembered for. If you can find a purpose for everything you do, your life will have meaning. If you have any regrets about things you wish you had done, now is the time to do them.

Barbara Sher, career counsellor and bestselling author, says "the fact that your awareness of mortality shows up at midlife is wonderful, because it pushes you as nothing else will into respecting your own happiness, and your happiness will unerringly draw you to your genius" (Sher, 1999).

Steven Pressfield, author of *The War of Art*, says, "Most of us have two lives. The life we live and the unlived life within us." What stops us living the second is procrastination or resistance. It is the force that prevents us from doing our work. He believes artists experience a freedom the rest of us fear. We are afraid to tackle a project that calls to us because it might compel us to explore unconscious parts of ourselves. It is the fear of what we might unleash when we follow our passion that can often hold us back.

Don't wait until your fear dissipates—walking through it is the only way to conquer it. The trick is to convince yourself to get started and just keep going. Serendipity will then come out to find you, and unseen forces will help you create. As the spiritual teacher, author, and lecturer Marianne Williamson wrote, we fear our success because it may force us to leave both our old self as well as others behind. We must find our path and follow it and do our work for its own sake to discover who we were meant to be.

My greatest fear was that I would not live up to my potential before I died. I choose to use my approaching death-clock, ticking away, to move forward with my desire to live my life on purpose. My office houses a small collection of glass and ceramic skulls as a gentle and amusing reminder.

Unreadable

Our subconscious mind never grows old. A comforting thought is that it is believed to survive death as it is part of the universal mind that connects us all. Old age does not destroy our creative powers. George Bernard Shaw was still active at ninety. It is only when we think old thoughts that we also act old. It is possible our later years are more enjoyable and productive than our younger years. Many before us have already proven this to be true. Michelangelo created some of his best paintings at eighty.

Embrace old age with a sense of grace and for the beauty, experience, and wisdom that accompany it. Use your age as the asset it is. People grow old when they lose interest in life and stop dreaming and searching for new paths to explore. When you no longer need to spend most of your time making a living, you will be free instead to create your life. Don't let society or the mass media define old age for you.

It was Napoleon Hill who first made me understand that "the entire world is made up of only two things: energy and matter. . . . Neither matter nor energy can be created nor destroyed. Both matter and energy . . . can be transformed, but neither can be destroyed. Life is energy. . . . Life cannot be destroyed. . . . Death is mere transition."

Begin with the end in mind
Keep this in mind when thinking about the legacy you'd like to leave behind. Perhaps you'd like to landscape a public area, fund a scholarship, or leave your land to a nature reserve. Will you have done most of what you wanted to do? Use your life in a meaningful way.

Many cultures throughout history have suggested we live every day as if death is close at hand. Some visualize it as a bird on their shoulder. My skull collection reminds me to live each day as if it were my last. One of my favourite sayings over the past few years has been: "The clock is ticking"—meaning, of course, that I had better get doing everything I really want to do. This thinking, though, can lead you to feel rushed and panicked.

What's Your Mission?

After I began meditating, I realized there was a better way to live. I now slow down and relax. I can watch a spider weave a web for hours and be utterly absorbed in the moment. There's no need to rush. Consciously choose to reduce your usual speed. Slowing down in a conscious manner empowers you to step out of the rush of your own surging thoughts and feelings. Cultivate a quiet mind. Sit in silence whenever you can. To go quiet, you must go within. To find what is timeless, live as though you have all the time in the world.

We talk about the seasons of life, but do we really understand what they mean? We Boomers have entered our third season, the time we should be getting ready to harvest the gifts we have sown and sharing our talents.

I'm afraid that plastic surgery, hair dye, botox, and our search for eternal youth are robbing us of the real gifts we have at this age. I'm certainly not against remaining healthy and vigorous and as good-looking as possible, for as long as we can. I just don't want us to paint the outside and find an empty box inside.

When Cynthia, a dear friend and former communal housemate from my twenties, died at the age of fifty-two, her death forced me to confront my own life.

North Americans don't want to look at death, especially their own—but doing so can help us celebrate and live the present moment more fully. Cynthia told me she wished she knew how much time she had left. It would help her set priorities and reassure her that she had enough money in the bank to support the rest of her journey.

After five years in remission, her cancer returned. Cynthia died three years ago. Writing this book was at the top of my "Bucket List." I hope it helps you not just to create your own Bucket List, but to live it.

This could be your last chance to be who you were meant to be. Don't wait any longer. Review the often-quoted words of

Marianne Williamson, "Your playing small does not serve the world . . . as we let our own light shine, we unconsciously give other people permission to do the same."

Edgar Cayce may have been right that we'll get another opportunity in another lifetime, but let's not take that chance. I tend to be a bit of a procrastinator. Many of us are. I don't want to be waiting for my possible reincarnation in order to live my dreams.

My father put many of his own dreams on hold while he raised his family. After all the kids left home, he envisioned paying off the mortgage and then he and my mother would drive across Canada from Ontario to explore the West Coast. He planned to retire at age sixty. He died at fifty-seven. Can you afford to wait for someday?

Action Steps – Questions to Ponder

Draw a Timeline with all the important events in your life on it:

- Start at birth and draw the line horizontally to age 100.
- Place a vertical line starting at age 10, 20, 30, and so on.
- Place an "x" where your current age is on the horizontal line.
- Indicate the highlights of your life at the 10-year marks.
- Consider the emotional impact of each event.
- Record a phrase that summarizes each one.
- If you believe you will live to 100, how much time do you have left?
- Write down what you'd like to accomplish between now and then.

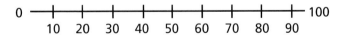

Here is how to create a more visual representation of this exercise:

Create a Mandala of Your Life

- Draw a circle on a large piece of cardboard with a clock face on it.
- At the 1 o'clock position, mark Age 10, at the 2 o'clock position, Age 20, and so forth, until you reach 12 o'clock which you can label Age 120 (since many are now living longer than Age 100.) Pay particular attention to where your current age is located.
- Paste pictures or symbols of the important highlights of your life in each pie-shaped segment. In the segments after your current age, indicate what you would like to experience in the future. Second-guess when your own death might occur. Place a star there. This represents the amount of time you think you have left.
- The clock is ticking—what do you plan to do with the time you have left?

Describe how you will work on your own terms.

What do you really want?

You might want to create a separate Vision Board in pictures that summarizes the words you've recorded in the previous chapters.

Visualize your dream attained:

- What does it look like?
- Focus on it daily and gradually your subconscious mind will go to work to achieve it.
- Be totally committed to achieving your goal.
- Maintain your focus.
- Keep your eye on the end result. This will help you over any hurdles you encounter along the way. There will be hurdles.
- Remember: this is your own Hero's Journey.

What do you consider to be your life's work?

It will flow naturally from your core values, interests, and talents. It will energize and help you feel fulfilled.

Blackboard Project Spreading Around the World

I've read about a popular local interactive art project that asks people to consider their final wishes. The project takes the form of an eight-foot high chalkboard that asks passers-by to finish the sentence: Before I die, I want to . . .

The idea originated on the side of an abandoned building in New Orleans and is now on walls in nearly fifty cities worldwide.

Complete the statement yourself: Before I die, I want to . . .

Then do it!

Soundtrack

From the Movie Rocky Horror Picture Show

Don't dream it. Be it.
* Don't dream it. Be it...*

Books You Might Like to Read

A Return to Love
by Marianne Williamson

Life After Death
by Deepak Chopra

I Could Do Anything If Only I Knew What It Was
by Barbara Sher

It's Only Too Late If You Don't Start Now
by Barbara Sher

Also Google

Cynthia Brouse recorded her journey on a blog called: *The Clothesline Saga.* You can still check it out online.

Chapter 29:
Wise Words Before Leaving

The greater danger for most of us lies not in setting our aim too high and falling short, but in setting our aim too low and achieving our mark.

Michelangelo

*Now I become myself. It's taken
time, many years and places;
I have been dissolved and shaken,
Worn other people's faces.*

From the poem, *Transparency*
by May Sarton

Ken Budd wrote an article for AARP (American Association of Retired Persons) titled: *Escape Your Comfort Zone* (May 30, 2012). In it he said, "Whatever scares you, do it. Now. Escaping your comfort zone can make you happier, smarter, more confident, more grateful, and more satisfied with life." He also pointed out that you might discover you don't need as much money in the bank as you once thought in order to truly enjoy your life.

In her book, *The Top Five Regrets of the Dying*, Bronnie Ware, a former palliative care nurse in Australia, recorded what dying patients told her they most regretted. They said they wished they had lived life on their own terms, not taken life so seriously, spent more time with family and friends than at work, had fully expressed their true feelings, and had realized they could have deliberately chosen to live a happier and more fulfilling life.

When people reflected on their lives, a common refrain was that they had foolishly pretended to be someone they weren't. Depriving themselves of the joy and laughter they craved, they had lived a lie for the sake of keeping up appearances. It was often a fear of the process of changing that prevented them from living with authenticity.

Michael W. Wiederman wrote "Mortal Thoughts," for Scientific American Mind (July/August 2012). He said a close brush with death—our own, or a loved one—can prompt us to reassess our lives. He believes that consciously thinking about our mortality is both worthwhile and beneficial and can lead to a shift in personal values and goals.

He said those who pursue meaning in life are better able to handle their mortality than those who chase after material wealth. Confronting death head-on can shift one's priorities away from what money can buy to the things money can't buy—including spiritual growth.

A study of California earthquake survivors revealed that those who had most strongly feared they would die in the quake indicated a shift from extrinsic to intrinsic goals. Wiederman said a Belgian study of adults with an average age of seventy-five showed a similar result. The study participants who said they had satisfied their internal goals for self-development and spiritual growth were happier with the lives they had lived and less fearful of death than those who had primarily chased after external, material goals.

Do you think Weiderman is correct when he suggests that thinking about our mortality might help us better prepare for it, while at the same time, helping us re-evaluate our priorities? What greatly alleviated my own fear of dying was holding my mother's hand as she took her last breath. That afternoon she had unexpectedly emerged from a deep coma. She was back with my brother and me for about an hour. During that time she sipped a little chocolate milk, sang a little nonsense song about Winnie the Pooh, and told us how excited she was to be leaving as she had family and friends waiting to meet her on the other side. She then fell back into a coma and died a few hours later. It was very peaceful.

Leonardo da Vinci said, "As a well-spent day brings happy sleep, so a life well used brings a happy death." Many years ago, I remember reading a line from an East Indian author who said, "Today is a good day to die." Live each day as if it were your last, because one day it will be. Awareness of death forces us to confront the purpose and meaning of our existence.

What's your legacy? Your Mission Possible
Do you have a Bucket List? Have you started to act on it? Does it include a way to give back? The top two items on my list were to write this book and learn to play a musical instrument. The week I began writing the first chapter, I also started playing the ukulele. I'll be sixty this year. I thought it best to start at the top of my list in case I never make my way down to the bottom. I hope you've already started working through your own.

What do you care deeply about? Can you think of something you would love to do whether or not you were paid for it? Is there a cause you would be willing to place your life on the line for? I have an eighty-five-year-old friend, Jean, who says her cause is to preserve the pristine wilderness of British Columbia by preventing an oil pipeline from being extended to the coast. As an active member of the Raging Grannies, she is more than willing to speak up about what she believes in.

Do you have any hobbies you've been so immersed in that you've lost track of time? These may lead you to follow your passion and transform it into paid employment.

You don't want people to deliver a eulogy on your life that talks about the great potential you had but didn't fulfill. As you take steps to move toward your goal, your goal will start to move toward you through synchronicity, if you don't allow fear to stop you in your tracks. What's a rut? It's spinning your wheels over and over while going nowhere.

It's time to express your uniqueness. If you don't have critics, you are likely not doing anything worthwhile. Welcome the critics. They will help to keep you on your path, providing you don't detour and follow theirs. Trust yourself to make decisions that are right for you. If anyone says you are being selfish, tell them it would be selfish of you not to share your real gifts with the world.

Now is the time to take on your life's work. What do you imagine when you picture the good work that will outlive you?

The poet May Sarton speaks of the importance of having a sense of one's life's mission. She wrote that developing our creativity allows us to be in touch with our muse, the creative force in the world, which in turn channels our purpose. Having a purpose in life is essential for mental, physical, and emotional well-being.

Many women, after menopause, become more in touch with their inner wisdom and more open to expressing it. Many cultures celebrate the wisdom of the crone. As Mona Lisa Schulz puts it, "Menopause is not a dead-end journey into decline and oblivion; it's an opportunity to tap fully into the intuition network," allowing one to tap into the wealth of insight and information that intuition offers. Intuition is our internal compass. It will point to our own "true north."

If you don't have goals to strive for, you may be living life—as if you were one of the living dead. Symptoms may include boredom, living in the past, unwilling to learn anything new, experiencing guilt or regret, craving "bad news" stories, lacking ambition, and unwilling to share your gifts with others. However, if this is you, would you be reading this book? Be grateful to be alive. Now, go out there and do something wonderful!

Action Steps – Questions to Ponder

As the clock ticks off the minutes, and you draw closer to your Departure Date, what message does this date have for you?

Medical science tells us Boomer women can expect to live to eighty-five and men to eighty-three. If we start collecting a government pension between age sixty and seventy, that will give us a chance to do something meaningful that contributes to society with the time we have left.

What is your purpose?
Your purpose runs deep in your soul. It is something you can dedicate your life to. It is the thread that runs throughout your journey.

Is there anything you wish you'd done differently?
Can you do it now?

If you haven't yet done this, create a Soul Card that reflects your core values.
Carry it with you to remind you of your path.

Watch, or rewatch the movie, *The Bucket List.*
Then, create your own list of all the things you'd like to do before your final curtain call. Deliberately choose how to spend your time and energy.
Then, take action.

What's on your Bucket List?

List everything you'd like to do before you die.

Highlight the most important item.

Go and do it! *(That's how this book got written.)*
Ignore any feelings that tell you it can't be done.

Don't look at your list again until you complete your first priority.

When you think about the end of your life, how will you answer these questions?

Did I use my career in a way that truly tested me to see what I could create?

How did I contribute to making the world a better place?

Who did I help along the way?

It is the big choices we make that set our direction. It is the small steps we take that get us to our destination. As Studs Terkel has recommended, "Throw yourself, heart and soul, into something you love and give it your best effort!"

Do you have a favourite quote to live by? What is it?

Read it daily as a reminder.

This quote, which I shared earlier, is the one I choose to live by:

This time, like all times,
is a very good one,
if we but know what to do with it.

Ralph Waldo Emerson

Soundtrack

From the Movie *Life of Brian* (Monty Python)

"Always Look on the Bright Side of Life"

If life seems jolly rotten,
There's something you've forgotten!
And that's to laugh and smile and dance and sing.

Books You Might Like to Read

Will the Circle Be Unbroken?
by Studs Terkel (a meditation on death and dying)

The Top Five Regrets of the Dying
by Bronnie Ware

Life After Death
by Deepak Chopra

Also Google

www.MindingtheMind.com

www.BuzanCentres.com

VII.
THAT'S WHAT FRIENDS ARE FOR

Chapter 30:
We Can Go Further Together

Isolation is a dream killer . . . You need accountability. You need a group of people who care if you make it or not. That's how things get done.

Barbara Sher

The people you associate with and the environment you live in will likely have a strong influence on what you do. Success is not about going it alone. Know when to ask for help. No one can do it all, especially if the goal is self-employment. At some stage in life, everyone should work to derive at least part of their income from their entrepreneurial abilities. It is the best personal growth program there is.

Self-employment promotes self-development as it stretches your skills and abilities. It will test you and inspire you to do more and become more than you ever thought possible. It will help connect you with amazing people. Your business can become a tool for the change you want to see in the world.

I recommend you create or join a Success Team, as promoted by Barbara Sher. It will help you through the ups and downs and provide a group to celebrate your success with. If you prefer to look for a new job, rather than self-employment, a Success Team will provide you the opportunity to brainstorm and network. One of the entrepreneurs in the group might end up creating a position for you.

Do you know why wild geese fly in a V-pattern? I read this many years ago when I first embarked on workshop facilitation. It serves to remind me why I recommend teamwork when people are making a change in their lives. This is what scientists believe to be the reason.

As each bird flaps its wings, it creates an updraft for the bird immediately following. By flying in a V-formation, the whole flock can travel farther than if each bird flew alone. By travelling together in community, they can get where they are going more quickly and easily, because they are able to take turns uplifting one another. When the lead goose gets tired, it rotates back into the V-formation and another goose takes the lead. Geese honk from behind to encourage those up front to keep going.

This is how the best groups work together to help all get where they want to go. Social interaction is good for keeping you focused on what you want, exchanging ideas, and enjoying the company of others. It also contributes to healthy aging.

Work with people who respect your knowledge and abilities and who can help you grow. You may need to seek out a new group of friends. Consider this: if you want to learn how to sail, you can't spend all of your time with landlubbers who are afraid of the water. Seek help from people who would like to learn along with you. Look for advice from people who have travelled down the path you'd like to follow. Some are in this book; others are likely in your neighbourhood or just a few keystrokes away via Google.

Few have created a successful business alone. Do the things you do best. Hire others to do what they do best. People are self-motivated when they are able to develop and use their favourite skills. The things you do best will energize you. Everything else will drain your energy. Think about how you can support others to achieve their goals.

The only way to grow is to stretch yourself. Set goals you are passionate about. Make sure they are in alignment with your core values and that they are at least slightly out of your current reach. This will keep you motivated to move toward them. Enjoy the process of moving forward.

The people you associate with are likely to help shape who you are. Make a conscious decision about who to surround yourself with while remembering a quote from Plato to "be kind along the way, for everyone you meet is fighting a hard battle." However, trust yourself to make the most important decisions in your life.

Ask successful people for advice. This book has explored the advice I've been given through the books I've read, people I've met, and through personal experience. Read books about successful people. Your local library will have a large selection of autobiographies and biographies to choose from. Successful people will want to help you. Ask one of them to mentor you. They can be older or younger than you. Start with the members of your local Chamber of Commerce. Helping you achieve success is a gift to myself. I want this world to be a better place for all of us.

Conquer your fear of rejection. You may hear "No" a lot before you hear the word "Yes." You could make a game of this. See how many times you can hear the word "No" before you do hear a "Yes." Do the thing you fear and the fear will disappear. This process may lead towards something much better than you antic-ipated.

It is your consistent choices that create your habits. Your habits determine your future. First, you need to be very clear about what you want. Write it out on a card you can carry with you and read it daily. Then, take action steps on a consistent basis to achieve it. Make a statement with your life that shows you've served a purpose and made a difference.

Action Steps – Questions to Ponder

Who would you like to ask to join your support team?

Who can you ask for advice?

Soundtrack

"With a Little Help from My Friends"
The Beatles

Oh, I get by with a little help from my friends.

Books You Might Like to Read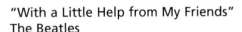

Teamworks!
by Barbara Sher

The Measure of a Man
by Sidney Poitier

I hope you will consider all the perspectives presented in this book and examine your own thoughts and beliefs, evaluate your life choices and then choose a conscious path for your own future. Step out of the mental prison you have created for yourself. Set yourself free. I believe we're here to better ourselves and to help each other.

When our work is done, we can leave in peace.

Chapter 31:
Write Your Next Chapter

The reasonable man adapts himself to the conditions that surround him. The unreasonable man adapts surrounding conditions to himself. All progress depends on the unreasonable man.

George Bernard Shaw

Now that you have spent thirty days with this book and completed all of the Action Steps, you can move forward with the Next Chapter of your life.

What did you learn about yourself while reading this book?

Has your mindset changed? Can you envision a positive future for yourself?

Have you created a clear picture of what you want?
Your Vision Board will serve as a visual reminder to move you forward.

It is not our feet that move us along—it is our minds.

Chinese proverb

If you could live your life based on your three favourite books— which books would you choose? Why?

How much income do you need each month to support your basic needs?

Where do you want to live? Describe your ideal life.

How will you develop your passion and creativity?

Which of your gifts do you most want to use?

Why do you want to perform your work?

Recall the words of Viktor Frankl:
"He who knows the 'why' of his existence
will be able to bear almost any 'how'."

Don't be afraid of making mistakes or being wrong—you'll learn and change directions, as needed.

What steps can you take right now?
Ask yourself this daily.

Focus on your desire
Visualize it. Review your Soul Card whenever you need to make a decision. Display your Vision Board where you can view it daily.

Stay focused on what you want.
The clock is ticking . . .
Enjoy the process of creating the life you want to lead.

Be open to serendipity
Once you start your journey and proceed in the direction you desire, serendipity will carry you along.

Soundtrack 🎵

"It's My Life"
Bon Jovi

It's my life,
It's now or never,
I ain't gonna live forever,
I just wanna live while I'm alive.

I've adopted "It's My Life" *as the theme song of my life.*

Choose a theme song for your own life.
Some of you may even want to write your own.
If you do, send me a YouTube version of it.

This acronym will help you remember the message of this book.

D = Desire—be clear about what you want.
R = Reduce your expenses in the short-term.
E = Engage your intuition, creativity and intention.
A = Awareness of your core values is essential.
M = Meaningful work is your focus.

Mindfulness must be engaged. Once there is seeing, there must be acting. Otherwise, what is the use of seeing?

Thich Nhat Hanh

Remember:

Choosing freedom can be a difficult choice because with it comes responsibility. When we allow others to have power over us, it can be an unconscious way to give ourselves permission to blame others for the way we live. Freedom is the right to make our own choices and to learn from them. Not everyone is ready for that kind of freedom.

Inner transformation always precedes a lasting outer change. I have heard that if you place a frog in a pot of water and set it on a stove to boil, the frog will not realize it should have jumped out until it is too late. Some people are like that frog. They will stick with what they know even if it is slowly killing them.

Don't be afraid to jump!

You've likely heard the saying "When one door closes, another door opens." The key is you must be willing to walk through it.

Soundtrack

The Hawaiian version of "Somewhere over the Rainbow," sung by the late, great Israel (IZ) Kamakawiwo'ole inspired me to learn to play the ukulele. This song repeatedly ran through my mind during the writing of this book.

Somewhere over the rainbow
Blue birds fly
And the dreams that you dreamed of
Dreams really do come true.

Stay focused and your dreams really will come true!

Jan

References

Adams, S. (1998). *The Dilbert Future.* New York: HarperBusiness.

Anderson, N. (2010). *Work with Passion in Midlife & Beyond.* Novato, CA: New World Library.

American Psychological Association.(March 8, 2011). APA Survey Finds Many U.S. Workers Feel Stressed Out and Undervalued. Retrieved from http://www.apa.org/news/press/releases/2011/03/ workers-stressed.aspx

Baker, N., Wolschin, F., Amdam, G. V. (2012). Age-related learning deficits can be reversible in honey bees apis mellifera. *Experimental Gerontology.* Retrieved from http://www.sciencedi-rect.com/science/article/pii/S0531556512001258

Banks, J., Nazroo, J., & Steptoe, A. (Eds.). (October 2012). The Dynamics of Ageing, Evidence from the English Longitudinal Study of Ageing, 2002-2010. Retrieved from http://www.ifs. org.uk/elsa/report12/elsaW5-1.pdf

Bronson, P. (2005). *What Should I Do With My Life?* New York: Ballantine Books.

Cahill, K. E., Giandrea, M. D., & Quinn, J. F. (May, 2012). Older Workers and Short-Term Jobs: Patterns and Determinants. *Monthly Labor Review.* Retrieved from http://www.bls.gov /opub/mlr/2012/05/art2exc.htm

Campbell, J. (2003). *The Hero's Journey.* Novato, CA: New World Library.

Canton, J. (2006). *The Extreme Future*. New York: Dutton-Penguin Group.

Cayce, H. L. (1964). *Venture Inward*. New York: Harper & Row.

CBC News Story. (April 27, 2011). 1/3 of retirees still in debt. *Statistics Canada*. Retrieved from http://www.cbc.ca/news/business/story/2011/04/27/business-retiree-debt.html

Chopra, D. (2006). *Life After Death*. New York: Harmony Books.

Council of Economic Advisors—Executive Office of The President. (March 2010). Work-Life Balance and the Economics of Workplace Flexibility. Retrieved from http://www.whitehouse.gov/files/documents/100331-cea-economics-workplace-flexibility.pdf

Covey, S. (1995). *First Things First*. New York: Fireside.

Craddock, M. (2004). *The Authentic Career*. Novato, CA: New World Library.

CSA Group. (2013). A Standard for Psychological Health and Safety in the Workplace. Retrieved from http://www.csa.ca/cm/ca/en/news/article/standard-for-psychological-health-and-safety-in-the-workplace

Csikszentmihalyi, M. (2007). *Flow: The Psychology of Optimal Experience*. New York: Harper Perennial.

Culp, K. J. (September 22, 2009). Baby Boomers Reinvent Retirement with Self-Employment. Retrieved from http://www.businessopportunity.com/Blog/baby-boomers-reinvent-retirement/

Das, R. (1971). *Be Here Now*. New York: Three Rivers Press.

Davis, J. (1999). 1,000 Marbles: A Little Something About Precious Time. Retrieved from http://www.landofmarbles.com/marbles-1000marbles.html

De Bono, E. (1980). *Future Positive.* Markham, ON: Penguin Books.

Dominguez, J., & Robin V. (1992). *Your Money or Your Life.* New York: Viking Penguin.

Dowd, C. (July 26, 2012). Tips for Boomers looking to launch their own business in Retirement. Retrieved from http://www.foxbusiness.com/personal-finance/2012/07/26/tips-for-boomers-looking-to-launch-their-own-business-in-retirement/

Duxbury, L. & Higgins, C. (2001). Work-Life Balance in the New Millennium: Where are we? Where do we need to go? *CPRN Discussion Paper No.W/12.* Retrieved from http://www.cprn.org/doc.cfm?doc=52&l=en

----------------------------.(2003). Work-Life Conflict in Canada in the New Millennium. *Final Report – October 2003.* Retrieved from http://publications.gc.ca/collections/Collection/H72-21-186-2003E.pdf

Dychwald, K. (2013). American's Perspectives on New Retirement Realities and the Longevity Bonus. A 2013 Merrill Lynch Retirement Study, Conducted in Partnership with *Age Wave (Dychwald).* Retrieved from http://wealthmanagement.ml.com/publish/content/application/pdf/GWMOL/2013_Merrill_Lynch_Retirement_Study.pdf

Dyer, W. (2009). *Change Your Thoughts, Change Your Life.* Carlsbad, CA: Hay House.

--------. (1999). *Manifest Your Destiny.* New York: HarperCollins.

--------. (2005). *The Power of Intention.* Carlsbad, CA: Hay House.

Emmons, R. (2013). The New Science of Gratitude. *Gratitude Power.* Retrieved from http://gratitudepower.net/science.htm

Ewing Marion Kauffman Foundation. (August 8, 2012). As Baby Boomers Reach Retirement, Many Turn to Entrepreneurship as Next Adventure. *News Release*. Retrieved from http://www.kauffman.org/newsroom/as-baby-boomers-reach-retirement-many-turn-to-entrepreneurship-as-next-adventure.aspx

Frankl, V. (1959). *Man's Search for Meaning*. New York: Pocket Books of Simon & Schuster.

Frederick, S. (2009). *I See Your Dream Job*. New York: St. Martin's Press.

Gardner, H. (1999). *Intelligence Reframed: Multiple Intelligences for the 21st Century*. New York: Basic Books.

Gilbert, E. (2006). *Eat. Pray. Love*. New York: Penguin Books.

Gordon, A. (January 16, 2013). Canada launches workplace standards for mental health and safety. Retrieved from http://www.thestar.com/news/world/2013/01/16/canada_launches_workplace_standards_for_mental_health_and_safety.html

Gurchiek, K. (September 15, 2010). Work/Life Balance Off-Kilter in U.S. *Society for Human Resource Management Survey*. Retrieved from http://www.shrm.org/Publications/HRNews/Pages/WorkLifeOffKilter.aspx

Hamilton, J. (November 11, 2005). The Links Between the Dalai Lama and Neuroscience. *NPR*. Retrieved from http://www.npr.org/templates/story/story.php?storyId=5008565

Haven, C. (October 13, 2010). Why the Dalai Lama comes to Stanford. *Stanford News*. Retrieved from http://news.stanford.edu/news/2010/october/ccare-tibetan-initiative-101310.html

Hill, N. (1937 – Public Domain). *Think and Grow Rich*. Meriden, Conn.: The Ralston Society.

Hipple, S. F. (September, 2010). Self-employment in the United States. *Monthly Labor Review.* Retrieved from http://www.bls.gov/opub/mlr/2010/09/art2full.pdf

Keyes, K. Jr. (1984). *The Hundredth Monkey.* Coos Bay, OR: Vision Books.

LaRochelle-Cote, S. (2010). Self-employment in the downturn. *Stats Canada Study. (March 2010—Perspectives).* Retrieved from http://www.statcan.gc.ca/pub/75-001-x/2010103/article/11138-eng.htm

Lipton, B. (2008). *Biology of Belief.* Carlsbad, CA: Hay House.

----------. (2009). *Spontaneous Evolution.* Carlsbad, CA: Hay House.

Lowe, G. (2000). *The Quality of Work.* Don Mills, ON: Oxford University Press.

---------. (2006). Human Solutions™ Report: Under Pressure. Implications of Work-Life Balance and Job Stress. Fall 2006. Retrieved from http://www.grahamlowe.ca/documents/182/Under%20Pressure%2010-06.pdf

Maté, G. (2004). *When the Body Says No.* Toronto, ON: Random House.

Marshall, K. (April 27, 2011). Retiring with debt. *Statistics Canada.* Retrieved from http://www.statcan.gc.ca/pub/75-001-x/2011002/article/11428-eng.htm

Maslow, A. H. (1968). *Toward a Psychology of Being.* New York: D. Van Nostrand.

Maw, J. Maslow and Manifesting Skills. *Good Vibe University.* Retrieved from http://www.goodvibeuniversity.com/public/Maslow.cfm

Maxwell, J. C. (2009). *How Successful People Think.* New York: Center Street— Hachette Book Group.

McLeod, S. A. (2007). Maslow's Hierarchy of Needs. Retrieved from http://simplypsychology.org/maslow.html

McTaggart, L. (2008). *The Field: The Quest for the Secret Force of the Universe.* New York: HarperCollins.

Millman, D. (2011). *The Four Purposes of Life.* Novato, CA: H J Kramer / New World Library.

Mipham, S. (2006). *Ruling Your World.* New York: Three Rivers Press.

Moore, J. L. (1999). *The Future of Work* (Thesis) Royal Roads University — Masters in Leadership and Training

Needleman, J. (1994). *Money and the Meaning of Life.* New York: Currency Doubleday.

Philips Index, United States Executive Report. (August, 2004). A National Study of Public Wellbeing. Retrieved from http://www.globalfuturist.com/images/docs/amsumm.pdf

Pink, D. H. (2006). *A Whole New Mind.* New York: Riverhead Books.

-----------. (2009). *Drive.* New York: Riverhead Hardcover.

-----------. (2002). *Free Agent Nation.* New York: Warner Books.

PR Newswire. (September 1, 2010). Amid Economic Woes, Americans Still Seriously Concerned About Work/Life Balance. *StrategyOne Public Opinion Survey.* Retrieved from http://www.prnewswire.com/news-releases/strategyone-public-opinion-survey-amid-economic-woes-americans-still-seriously-concerned-about-worklife-balance-101967318.html

Proctor, B. (1984). *You Were Born Rich.* Downloadable PDF. Retrieved from http://www.bobproctordownloads.com/BornRich Book.pdf

Richards, D. (1995). *Artful Work.* New York: A Berkley Book.

Rix, S. E. (2012). The Employment Situation, May 2012: Good News is Hard to Find. *AARP Public Policy Institute, Fact Sheet 260,* June 2012. Retrieved from http://www.aarp.org/work/job-hunting/info-06-2012/the-employment-situation-may-2012-AARP-ppi-econ-sec.html

Rouse, C. (March 31, 2010). The Economics of Workplace Flexibility (blog). *Council of Economic Advisers.* Retrieved from http://www.whitehouse.gov/blog/2010/03/31/economics-work-place-flexibility

Schulz, M. L. (1998). *Awakening Intuition.* New York: Three Rivers Press.

Schwartz, D. J. (1983). *The Magic of Getting What You Want.* New York: A Berkely Book.

Senge, P., Scharmer C.O., Jaworski J., & Flowers, B.S. (2005). *Presence.* New York: Currency/Doubleday.

Sher, B. (1999). *It's Only Too Late if You Don't Start Now.* New York: Dell.

Sher, B., & Smith, B. (1994). *I Could Do Anything If Only I Knew What It Was.* New York: Delacorte Press.

Sher, B., & Gottlieb, A. (1989). *Teamworks!* New York: Warner Books.

------------------------. (1979). *Wishcraft: How To Get What You Really Want.* New York: Ballantine Books.

Smith, C. (December 4, 2005). Servant Leadership: The Leadership Theory of Robert K. Greenleaf. Retrieved from http://www.carol-smith.us/downloads/640greenleaf.pdf

Tapscott, D. (2009). *Grown Up Digital*. New York: McGraw-Hill.

Taylor, J. B. (2006). *My Stroke of Insight*. New York: Viking Press.

Terkel, S. (1998). *Working*. New York: The New Press.

----------. (2002). *Will the Circle Be Unbroken?* New York: A Ballantine Book.

Tharp, T. (2003). *The Creative Habit*. New York: Simon & Schuster.

Tieger, P. D., & Barron-Tieger, B. (1992). *Do What You Are*. New York: Little, Brown & Company.

Tolle, E. (2008). *A New Earth*. New York: Plume.

-------. (2012). *The Power of Now*. Novato, CA: New World Library.

Ware, B. (2012). *The Top Five Regrets of the Dying*. Bloomington, IN: Balboa Press/ Hay House.

Weeks, D. (1995). *Eccentrics*. New York: Kodansha America.

Weil, Dr. A. (2007). *Healthy Aging*. New York: Anchor Books.

Williamson, M. (1996). *A Return to Love*. New York: HarperCollins.

Winter, B. J. (1993). *Making a Living Without A Job*. New York: Bantam Books.

Zelinski, E. J. (2009). *Career Success Without a Real Job*. Berkeley, CA: Visions International Publishing/Ten Speed Press.

--------------. (1994). *The Joy Of Not Knowing It All: Profiting from creativity at work or play.* Chicago: VIP Books.

--------------. (1991). *The Joy of Not Working.* Edmonton, Alberta: Visions International Publications.

Suggested Reading

Adams, Scott. (1998). *The Dilbert Future.* New York: HarperBusiness.

Albom, Mitch. (1997). *Tuesdays With Morrie.* New York: Doubleday.

Anderson, Greg. (1997). *Living Life on Purpose.* New York: HarperCollins.

Anderson, Joan. (2006). *A Weekend to Change Your Life.* New York: Broadway Books.

----------------. (2008). *The Second Journey.* New York: Hyperion Books.

Axline, Virginia. (1986). *Dibs In Search of Self.* New York: Ballantine Books.

Bellman, Geoffrey M. (1990). *The Consultant's Calling.* San Francisco, CA: Jossey-Bass Inc.

Bender, Peter Urs. (1997). *Leadership from Within.* Toronto, ON: Stoddart Publishing

Bissonnette, Denise. (1994). *Beyond Traditional Job Development: The Art of Creating Opportunity.* Chatsworth, CA: Milt Wright & Assoc.

Boldt, Laurence G. (1999). *Zen and the Art of Making a Living.* New York: Penguin Books.

Bolles, Richard Nelson. (2011). *What Color is Your Parachute?* Berkeley, CA: Ten Speed Press. (Updated annually since 1970.)

Brand, Stewart. (1972) *The Whole Earth Catalog.* Menlo Park, CA: Portola Institute.

Bridges, William. (1997). *Creating You & Co. Reading, MA: Addison-Wesley.*

Bronson, Po. (2005). *What Should I Do With My Life?* New York: Ballantine Books.

Buffet, Mary. (2006). *The Tao of Warren Buffett.* New York: Scribner.

Cameron, Julia. (2002). *The Artist's Way.* New York: Tarcher/Putnam.

Campbell, Joseph. (2003). *The Hero's Journey.* Novato, CA: New World Library.

Canfield, Hansen & Hewitt. (2000). *The Power of Focus.* Deerfield Beach, FL: Health Communications Inc.

Carroll, Lewis. (2008). *Alice in Wonderland.* London, GB: HarperCollins.

Cayce, Hugh Lynn. (1964). *Venture Inward.* New York: Harper & Row.

Chopra, Deepak. (2006). *Life After Death.* New York: Harmony Books.

Craddock, Maggie. (2004). *The Authentic Career.* Novato, CA: New World Library.

Cutler, Howard C. & H H Dalai Lama. (1998). *The Art of Happiness.* New York: Riverhead Books.

Das, Ram. (1971). *Be Here Now.* New York: Three Rivers Press.

De Bono, Edward. (1980). *Future Positive.* Markham, ON: Penguin Books.

Dominguez, Joe & Vicki Robin. (1992). *Your Money or Your Life.* New York: Viking Penguin.

Dyer, Wayne. (2004). *The Power of Intention.* Carlsbad, CA: Hay House.

Edwards, Paul & Sarah. (2007). *Middle Class Lifeboat.* Nashville, TN: Thomas Nelson Inc.

Elgin, Duane. (1981). *Voluntary Simplicity.* New York: Bantam Books.

Everett, Melissa. (1995). *Making a Living While Making a Difference.* New York: Bantam Books.

Finley, Guy. (1995). *Designing Your Own Destiny.* St. Paul, MN: Llewellyn Publications.

Frankl, Viktor. (1959). *Man's Search for Meaning.* New York: Pocket Books of Simon & Schuster.

Frederick, Sue. (2009). *I See Your Dream Job.* New York: St. Martin's Press.

Friedan, Betty. (1994). *The Fountain of Age.* New York: Simon & Schuster.

Furst, Jeffrey, Editor. (1972). *Edgar Cayce's Story of Attitudes and Emotions.* New York: A Berkley Book.

Grube, G. M. A. (1992 Translation). *Plato: Republic.* Indianapolis, IN: Hackett Publishing Co.

Guillebeau, Chris. (2012). *The $100 Startup.* New York: Crown Business.

Harner, Michael. (1990 ed.). *The Way of the Shaman.* New York: HarperCollins.

Hawkins, James. For a copy of *My Private Parts* by James Hawkins, contact Bliss Publications: gabriolablisspublications@yahoo.ca

Helmstetter, Shad. (1989). *Choices.* New York: Pocket Books.

Hemingway, Ernest. (1964). *A Moveable Feast.* New York: Collier Books

Hubbard, Barbara Marx. (2012). *Birth 2012 and Beyond.* Chicago, IL: Shift Books/ipg.

------------------------. (1976). *The Hunger of Eve.* Mechanicsburg, PA: Stackpole Books.

Keen, Sam. (1992). *Fire in the Belly.* New York: Bantam Books.

Lipton, Bruce. (2008). *Biology of Belief.* Carlsbad, CA: Hay House.

---------------. (2009). *Spontaneous Evolution.* Carlsbad, CA: Hay House.

Lonely Planet Travel Guides (Select by country).

Lowe, Graham S. (2000). *The Quality of Work.* Don Mills, ON: Oxford University Press.

Mason, Bruce. (2012). *Our Clinic: Visionary Health Care, Fundraising and Community Building on Gabriola Island.* Gabriola, BC: Words@Work.

Maté, Gabor. (2004). *When the Body Says No.* Toronto, ON: Random House/Printorioum Bookworks.

Mayes, Frances. (1997). *Under the Tuscan Sun.* San Francisco, CA: Chronicle Books.

Mayes, Peter. (1989). *A Year in Provence.* New York: Vintage Books.

McTaggart, Lynne. (2008). *The Field: The Quest for the Secret Force of the Universe.* New York: HarperCollins.

Myss, Carolyn. (1998). *Why People Don't Heal and How They Can.* New York: Three Rivers Press.

Needleman, Jacob. (1994). *Money and the Meaning of Life.* New York: Currency/ Doubleday.

O'Hara, Bruce. (1994). *Put Work in Its Place.* Vancouver, BC: New Star Books.

Patterson, Freeman. (1979). *Photography and the Art of Seeing.* New York: Van Nostrand Reinhold.

Peck, M. Scott. (1997). *The Road Less Traveled and Beyond.* New York: Touchstone.

Pink, Daniel H. (2009). *Drive.* New York: Riverhead Hardcover.

----------------. (2002). *Free Agent Nation.* New York: Warner Books.

Poitier, Sidney. (2007). *The Measure of a Man.* San Francisco, CA: Harper.

Pressfield, Steven. (2003). *The War of Art.* New York: Grand Central Publishing.

Richards, Dick. (1995). *Artful Work.* New York: A Berkley Book.

Rubin, Gretchin. (2009). *The Happiness Project.* New York: HarperCollins.

Schulz, Mona Lisa. (1998). *Awakening Intuition.* New York: Three Rivers Press.

Schwartz, David J. (1983). *The Magic of Getting What You Want.* New York: A Berkely Book.

Senge, Peter, Claus Otto Scharmer, Joseph Jaworski & Betty Sue Flowers. (2005). *Presence.* New York: Currency/Doubleday.

Sher, Barbara. (1999). *It's Only Too Late if You Don't Start Now.* New York: Dell.

Sher, Barbara & Barbara Smith. (1994). *I Could Do Anything If Only I Knew What It Was.* New York: Delacorte Press.

Sher, Barbara & Annie Gottlieb. (1991). *Teamworks!* New York: Warner Books.

Shuman, Michael H. (2007). *The Small-Mart Revolution.* San Francisco, CA: Berrett–Koehler Publishing.

Sirolli, Ernesto. (1999). *Ripples From The Zambezi.* Gabriola, BC: New Society Publishers.

Tapscott, Dan. (2009). *Grown Up Digital.* New York: McGraw-Hill.

Terkel, Studs. (1998). *Working.* New York: The New Press.

--------------. (2002). *Will the Circle Be Unbroken?* New York: A Ballantine Book.

Tharp, Twyla. (2003). *The Creative Habit.* New York: Simon & Schuster.

Tieger, Paul D. & Barbara Barron-Tieger. (1992). *Do What You Are.* New York: Little, Brown & Company.

Tolle, Eckhart. (2012). *The Power of Now.* Novato, CA: New World Library.

Wakan, Naomi Beth. (2006). *Late Bloomer.* Hamilton, ON: Wolsak and Wynn.

----------------------. (2007). *Ageing.* Toronto, ON: Bevalia Press.

----------------------. (2008). *A Gabriola Year.* Toronto, ON: Bevalia Press.

Warren, Rick. (2002). *The Purpose Driven Life.* Grand Rapids, Mich.: Zondervan Books.

Weeks, David. (1995). *Eccentrics.* New York: Kodansha America.

Weil, Dr. Andrew. (2007). *Healthy Aging.* New York: Anchor Books.

Wheatley, Margaret J. (1992). *Leadership and the New Science.* San Francisco: Berrett-Koehler Publishing.

Williamson, Marianne. (1996). *A Return to Love.* New York: HarperCollins.

Winter, Barbara J. (1993). *Making a Living Without A Job.* New York: Bantam Books.

Woods, Emma. (2010). *A Brit Different.* London, UK: Punk Publishing Ltd.

Zukav, Gary. (1990). *Seat of the Soul.* New York: Fireside.

About The Author

Jan is a playful and engaging workshop facilitator with more than twenty years' experience in career counselling.

She has an MA in Leadership and Training, numerous certificates in counselling, diplomas in Corporate Communications and Recreation Leadership, is a qualified instructor of the Myers-Briggs Type Indicator and is certified in three areas: Life Skills Coach, Senior Advisor, and Retirement Coach.

Jan facilitates Retreats to guide women through the process of living and working on their own terms. Music and laughter are always included.

She lives with her husband, Tony, and their little dog, Newman, surrounded by creative artists of all types in an idyllic setting on one of the West Coast Gulf Islands. Her love of music often has her out Morris Dancing, singing in a choir, or playing out-of-tune songs on her ukulele.

Please visit www.WorkOnYourOwnTerms.com to download a Free copy of Jan's eBook: ***Create Career Joy!*** *Resources to Discover Your Dream Work (10 Steps to Create Your Plan for the Future).*

To order copies of the printed or eBook version of
Work On Your Own Terms,
please contact the publisher at
Jan@WorkOnYourOwnTerms.com

Royal Roads University Supports Midlife Learners

I have deep gratitude for my education at Royal Roads University. I completed my MA in Leadership & Training in 1999. *Work On Your Own Terms* is a follow-up to my thesis, *The Future of Work*.

This is why I recommend RRU for continued training in midlife:

- You will learn as much about yourself as about your field of study.
- The geographic location itself is spectacular. It has a Castle on the ocean, a lagoon, many woodland trails, plus a garden (historic Hatley Park) that ranges from Italian to Japanese.
- The university is responsive to student input.
- The programs allow for 'real world' applied research.
- Each program is designed with midlife learners in mind.
- Distance learning is combined with on-campus residencies where you collaborate on projects with other midlife learners.
- There is a wide range of programs to choose from.
- You can continue to work while you learn.
- Admission requirements include your passion and commitment along with your prior learning – both formal and informal.
- International students increase exposure to other cultures.
- You are taught by professionals with real-world experience.
- You can implement your new knowledge immediately.
- You will join the growing list of graduates who are out to change the world for the better.